"Now Who Are You?"

Identity Revealed

Joe Nicola

2019

"Now Who Are You?"
Identity Revealed

Copyright © 2019 — Joe Nicola

All rights reserved. This book is protected by the copyright laws of the United States of America. This book may not be copied or reprinted for commercial gain or profit. The use of short quotations or occasional page copying for personal or group study is encouraged. Permission will be granted upon request from Joe Nicola. Unless otherwise stated, all biblical quotations are taken from the 1995 version New American Standard Bible. All rights reserved. Any emphasis added to Scripture quotations is the author's own.

First Printing: 2019

ISBN: 9781463763138

Cover design by Joe Nicola

Editing and typesetting by Jim Bryson

(JamesLBryson@gmail.com)

Copy Edit by Renee Nicola and Mae Beach

ENDORSEMENTS

As a psychologist, in the cases that I encounter, identity plays a major part in the issues being addressed. All are experiencing some sort of an identity crisis. The absolute truth of one's identity brings about a mindset that is life-changing and rewarding. Joe Nicola's book on Identity is an exploration that proceeds deeply into our true identity; more than just the everyday surface discussions that we engage in. It extends beyond a natural view and submerses you into the discovery of who God truly created you to be—the discovery of your God-given identity. Misconceptions, misinterpretations and myths are all laid to rest here. It is only upon this revelation that you will find your true purpose, calling and discover the true meaning of living. This book is a must-read both for those who are just beginning their walk with Christ and for those who are seasoned.

    Dr. Brenda Craven, Ph.D.
    Psychologist and Pastoral Care NCM

*****

I've known Joe Nicola for 20 years. He is a man of integrity, who lives his convictions. His book on identity is an arrow piercing the heart, revealing our greatest need to know who we really are. This book will bring healing and restoration to lost identity.

    Regina Shank Global
    Transformation International

*****

When a mighty tree spreads itself in the forest, you know that its root structure goes far deeper than what is seen above ground. So it is with God's message of our identity. In Joe Nicola's book, *Now Who Are You?*, I hear reverberations of the same message that is flowing through me and many others. It is good to know we are not alone nor off on some personal agenda. We are one body, hearing one Lord, and we are speaking from a variety of God-given perspectives. We are functioning in our Identity as sons and daughters of God.

Bless you, Joe, for this work and for the many to come.

>Clay Nash, Apostle
>Network of Ekklesia International
>Olive Branch, Mississippi

*****

If we have a distorted or improper image of God, we will have a distorted self-image and a flawed identity. If you are struggling with identity issues that are confounding your self-worth, this book will put you on the path to truly understand whom you are AND why this exercise is so important. Joe Nicola takes the concept of "Be yourself" to a level most of us have never embraced before but he shows us all how to get there.

>Joey Knight
>FCBH

*****

My great friend Joe Nicola shares a wealth of wisdom, experience and insight to help the body of Christ grow in their identity and in spiritual maturity. This book is a summary of a pastor, leader and life-long learner. If you have a longing to grow closer to Jesus Christ this book will be food for your soul and a practical guide for your own journey.

>Pastor Gary Schmitz
>Executive Director
>Citywide Prayer Movement Kansas City
>Founder-Board Chairman Caring for Kids Network

*****

Joe Nicola's new book entitled *Now Who Are You?* is in my opinion the most important subject in the Body of Christ today. He has done a masterful job with this subject and included key scriptures throughout this work. I was personally greatly impacted as I read portions of it, through tear filled eyes.

>Michael Lazio
>Senior Pastor of Bethel House of Prayer

Table of Contents

Introduction xi

Preface xv

1. "Now Who Are You?" 1

2. Man's Greatest Need 7

3. What Is Man? 27

4. Identification 35

5. The Man Jesus 49

6. A New Creation 69

7. Adoption 93

8. What's In A Name? 109

9. My Beloved 115

10. Changing Our Mindset 123

11. Dominion 145

For Further Reading 159

Contact Information 161

Dedication

I DEDICATE THIS BOOK first to my wife, Renee, who has always encouraged me and stood by my side. She has been patient as I have journeyed to discover who I am. Renee, you are my gift from God. I am so thankful He brought us together!

To my friends who took their time to read this manuscript and write an endorsement: Thank you!

To my congregation, that puts up with me and encourages me. It is an honor to serve side by side with you! Thank you!

Finally, to my Savior and King, Jesus! There are not enough words to express my gratitude for who you are and all you have done!

Introduction

In 2004, approximately 6 million people in the United States alone were the victims of identity theft. And in 2017, there were over 15 million identity theft victims. That's nearly one every two seconds. This resulted in an estimated total cost to Americans of $53 billion, an approximate loss of $3,500 per person! The epidemic problem of identity theft carries a prophetic message we cannot ignore.

In addition to identity theft, we are faced with gender confusion. When people do not even know if they are male or female by their created biological uniqueness, we have a major identity crisis on our hands. Businesses are allowing men and women, boys and girls, to use the same restrooms and fitting rooms. Some school districts around the country are allowing biological boys who "identify" as a girl use the girl's locker room and vice versa. Yes, we have a serious identity problem!

As the people of God, we understand and accept that unbelievers have had their God-given identities stolen. But even more alarming is the fact that many Christians have also had their God-given identities stolen. Even as identity theft in America and around the world has resulted in both an individual and a shared cost to our lives, so too the Body of Christ suffers loss when we do not understand and walk in our individual and mutual God-given identity.

In their search for identity, many people today are interested in discovering their ancestral roots. Here in Independence, Missouri, we have the largest freestanding genealogy library in the United States. Many Christians are seeking to find their Jewish or Hebrew roots. You cannot turn your TV on without seeing a commercial for DNA testing.

Yes, discovering our history and ancestry has become big business with TV shows, genealogical clubs, internet and social media sites devoted to helping others discover their heredity. Ancestry.com, the largest online website devoted to helping people discover their ancestral roots, was sold for $1.6 billion dollars in 2012.

There are many theories about the beginning of mankind and his existence, evolution being the most popular. Three age-old questions still plague people:

Who am I?

Why am I here?

Where am I going?

These are vital questions that God has placed in the human heart, and we must find true answers for them. If we arrive at the correct answer to who am I, it will help guide us to the answers of the other two questions. Knowing the truth of our identity and origin defines who and what we are, how we are to live, and what we are to do. It also reveals the answer to what happens when we die.

The Bible records in Genesis 3 that the serpent confronted Eve in the Garden of Eden. He was successful in deceiving her so that she not only believed a lie about

God but in so doing, she came to believe a lie about herself. The serpent called the character of God into question by telling Eve that God knew that when she ate the fruit of the forbidden tree, her eyes would be opened and she would "be like God." In other words, the serpent insinuated that God was holding out on her, keeping something "good" from her.

When Adam and Eve ate from the tree, the serpent succeeded in hijacking their God-given identity. As a result, an orphan spirit was released. The orphan spirit is a result of fatherlessness. Man went from receiving their identity from their true Father, the God of all creation—and therefore receiving their value and self-worth—to searching for it in the world.

From Genesis 3, we learn a foundational truth: When we believe a lie about the nature of God and His character, we open ourselves to deception about our own identity. Our self-discovery of our own identity can only be seen through the lens of the identity of God the Father. If we have a distorted image of God, this leads us to a distorted image of our selves.

In this book, we will journey through the Scriptures to discover the meaning of our new identity, specifically who and what we are. We will illuminate truths that will recover and restore our God-given identity and purpose.

> *Therefore from now on we recognize no one according to the flesh; even though we have known Christ according to the flesh, yet now we know Him in this way no longer. Therefore if anyone is in Christ, he is a new creature; the old*

> *things passed away; behold, new things have come.*
>
> 2 Corinthians 5:16-17

What we believe about our self determines what we finally become and therefore predicts how we will behave and how we will treat others. If we believe we are a failure and good for nothing, we will travel a downward road and never reach the potential God has planned for us. On the other hand, if we believe and receive what God says about us, we will travel a road of blessing and power and live a life of purpose we have only dreamed of. It is a matter of living life from a place of being and not striving to become. It is really up to us. Which will we choose?

I began to write this book back in 2001. At that time, I decided to keep it concise and use it more as a study guide for my own congregation. As I gained more revelation on the subject, however, I expanded it over the years to what is now this book. My hope is that this book will help us to receive the truth of who and what we are and all that God says about us, and then choose to believe and live accordingly. Any lie that we have believed is overcome by the truth. We must know the truth and the truth will set you free (John 8:32).

When referring to identity, I am speaking of the essence of *who* we are—the *what* we are. The essence, nature and substance that makes us what God created us to be as human beings with a focus on the change to our nature that occurs when we are born again. Although worthy of discussion, I am not referring to the aspect of our identity that speaks of what we do for an occupation or the gifts we function in that God has given us as part of His Body.

July 1994, I liquidated my motorcycle shop. Standing in the midst of a dismantled business, feeling confused, lost and wondering what I was going to do next, God spoke. He asked me a question—one that impacted me deeply and I will never forget. He asked, *"Now who are you?"*

The quest to discover the answer to that question has been a journey. It is the result of this book.

Preface

IDENTITY

i·den·ti·ty, [ˌīˈden(t)ədē] The distinguishing character, nature and essence, including the personality of an individual. A state of being. The condition of being the same with something or someone. The relation established by psychological identification. The fact of being who or what a person or thing is.

The Hebrew word for identity is זהות

(Reading right to left)

ז - Zayin; #7 - A picture of a sword. Represents the spirit. The spirit that activates the physical.

ה - Hey; #5 - A picture of a man with arms raised. The breath of God. Divine revelation. The essence of life in all creation.

ו - Nun; #50 - A picture of a seed. Faithfulness. Represents the soul, a son and an heir. The ability to increase and multiply.

ת - Tav; #400 - A picture of crossed sticks. Represents a sign, monument or mark.

DEOXYRIBONUCLEIC ACID

DNA or deoxyribonucleic acid is the hereditary material in humans and almost all other organisms. It is known as the building block of life. The information in DNA is stored as a code made up of four chemical bases;

nitrogen bases are adenine (A), thymine (T), guanine (G) and cytosine (C). The order of these bases is what determines DNA's instructions, or genetic code. Human DNA has around 3 billion bases, and more than 99 percent of those bases are the same in all people, according to the U.S. National Library of Medicine.

THE ORPHAN SPIRIT

Adam and Eve's sin in the Garden of Eden resulted in fatherlessness being released in the earth. Fatherlessness produces an orphan spirit that causes feelings of abandonment, rejection, isolation and loneliness. The orphan spirit causes one to give themselves over as a slave. I am not defining one who has been forced into slavery but one who gives himself up to the will of another as Adam and Eve did. As scripture says, we become slaves to the one we obey. Israel possessed a slave mentality when Moses led them out of Egypt. Instead of receiving God as Father and King, they wanted to return to slavery in Egypt to get their needs met. Fatherlessness and the orphan spirit permeate the world.

SONS OF GOD

Jesus said, "You search the Scriptures because you think that in them you have eternal life; it is these that testify about Me..." (John 5:39). Scripture, both Old (First) and New (Second) Covenants, is the revelation of the Son of God—Jesus. This revelation leads us to the revelation of the sons of God, the children of God, the Ekklesia as a family dynasty.

1

"Now Who Are You?"

For as a he (man) *thinks within himself, so he is.*
Proverbs 23:7 (parenthesis added)

I WAS RAISED ON LONG ISLAND, New York until my parents divorced when I was twelve. My mother, two sisters, a brother-in-law and myself moved to Independence, Missouri, where my grandparents lived. My father and my older brother remained in New York. The divorce was difficult on me, as it is with most children at that age. Not having my dad around, being some 1,300 miles away, was very difficult.

After four years and a sophomore in High School, I moved back with my father and his new wife. A year later I was back in Missouri living with my mother and her new husband. I attempted to finish High School but didn't make it. After returning to school following the Christmas break of my junior year, I lasted about a month and was kicked out, never to return. I experimented with marijuana at the age of 13 and advanced to alcohol and then hard drugs. I kept up that destructive lifestyle until the age of 20. As I progressed through my teen years, I made many wrong choices, even illegal choices. I never felt like I fit in anywhere. I had a need for belonging, but I was hurt and angry inside and didn't know what to do about it except alleviate the pain any way possible.

In July 1981, at the age of 17, I attended a four-month trade school in Daytona Beach, Florida to learn motorcycle repair with my girlfriend, Renee (now my wife). Two years later, during the winter of 1983—a time when Renee and I had broken off the relationship—I visited my father and step-mother for Christmas. While there, I had an encounter with the living God.

Jehovah's Witnesses came to the door one day. (Note: I am not a Jehovah's Witness, but I do witness for Jehovah.) They were selling the Watch Tower magazine. I liked the mushroom cloud of the nuclear explosion on the front cover, so I gave them a few bucks and went to shut the door. They said, "wait, let us give you this book." It was a little green book that read *Family Living* on the front cover. I thumbed through the magazine looking for other cool pictures, that took about 30 seconds. I started reading the book at night in my bedroom and I found my heart longing for family the way God created it to be.

One night the Lord showed up! I didn't know it was Him at the time. All I knew was that He held me in His arms as if I was a small child. For the first time in my life I experienced unconditional love beyond what any human can give. I thought for a moment it might be a hallucination from too many drugs. But no, it was real, genuine and like nothing I have ever experienced before. I really wasn't sure what was going on, but I liked it! It was almost too wonderful to be true, but it was!

This encounter with God and His unconditional love for me changed my life forever! This was the moment of my new birth. I was born again (John 3), even though I didn't know that at the time either. Despite the fact that I had drugs on me, God still accepted me, loved me and was very affectionate toward me. He didn't tell me that He would love me if I quit doing drugs and flush the cocaine down the toilet. No, He didn't reference my sin at all! Instead, His love melted away my addiction over time. He is such a great, loving and caring Daddy.

At the moment of that encounter, I knew for the first time in my life what I was supposed to do. I didn't know how I knew; I just knew that I was to go back to Missouri, get a job and ask Renee (who at the time didn't want anything to do with me) to marry me. It was going to be an awkward moment (to say the least)—she was really fed up with me. But we were married six months later on June 2, 1984.

Actually, 1984 was a banner year for me. I got born again, proposed to Renee, married her, joined the Navy and left for basic training on my 21st birthday...all in 1984.

After completing my active duty in the Navy and based on my several years' experience working in various motorcycle dealerships, I started my own business in the Spring of 1986—Vision Cycles, a motorcycle parts and repair shop. I was now a motorcycle mechanic and business owner, and I took great pride in that. I didn't realize it at the time that I was finding my self-worth in my occupation. I felt valued and that made me feel good about myself.

At the age of 31, the Lord began a change in me, and I knew I had to answer a call to sell my business and go into full-time youth ministry. At the time, I didn't realize how hard it would be to sell my business—partly because it didn't sell! I had one buyer but that fell through. So I was forced to liquidate my tools and equipment piece by piece. Looking back on it, I realize that God was taking me on a journey to do a deep work in my heart. At the time, however, it hurt beyond words. With every piece of equipment sold, there was a story of how God provided the money for it or created the deal through which I purchased it. Oh, the memories…so many memories. Every item that was sold and left the building was one more repair I wouldn't be able to accomplish on a motorcycle. Piece by piece my heart was being torn to pieces. Letting faithful employees go was difficult as well.

> *Piece by piece, my heart was being torn to pieces.*

I felt lost and insecure. So many thoughts raced through my mind. Now what am I going to do? The only way I knew how to make a living was gone. Fear gripped me time after time. My mind raced. How was I going to make a decent living? How was I going to provide for my wife, pay the house payment and utilities, put food on the table? Questions…many questions. Ok, near panic!

In July of 1994, with little left in my motorcycle shop, I heard the voice of God within me ask a question I will never forget, *"Now who are you?"*

Who am I? That question rocked me! *Who am I?* I didn't even know what I was doing, where I was going or what I was going to do next, much less who I was. *Who am I?* I don't know!

I obviously didn't know how to answer that question. I certainly wasn't who I thought I was. I was a business owner and a motorcycle mechanic, and that was being torn from me. Sure, I was still a husband with a great wife. I was even a part-time youth pastor. But my career! My business! What I invested so much time, sweat, money and effort to build...was gone! Gone!

I didn't realize at the time that I was receiving something deep within me from my business. I was getting a need met and didn't even know it. I didn't know this was happening until it was gone. Boy, did I know something was missing then! Through the Lord's question, I discovered that I found my identity in my title and my occupation. I was receiving value and self-worth from these temporary things. I had no idea I was doing this! Even if I did know it, I wouldn't have thought it was wrong. When I was discharged from the Navy in 1990, it didn't have the same effect on me as my business did. The same with being a youth pastor when I left that position in the summer of 1999. The reason for that is I wasn't finding my identity from the Navy or from being a youth pastor, but I was from being a motorcycle mechanic and business owner.

Who Am I?

This set me on a journey of discovery. It took a while—years even. I learned that properly framing a question leads to the answer. Here are a few questions I wrestled with during the journey.

- When we no longer can do what we are doing, who are we?
- When we no longer possess what we had, who are we?

- When we no longer have the title before our name, who are we?
- When all our children have grown and moved out of the house, who are we?
- When we age and grow older and we literally cannot do what we did before, who are we?
- When all is stripped away and we are standing there alone, who are we?

We must understand one fundamental thing: We are not what we do. Our value and worth do not come from our bank accounts. We are not the sum total of our possessions. Sure, we can enjoy all these things but our identity, and therefore our value and worth, must come from something much deeper.

On this journey to discover who I am, I found something that I didn't expect—something deep and life-changing. I came to understand the love that Father God has for me in a deeper way than I had encountered before. I became a "beloved son." Not from God's perspective—He already loved me like that. No, the change was in my perspective. Now I knew it! I knew how He loved me, that I was truly His son, that His love was profound, abiding and eternal. I became His beloved son in my heart.

I believe the same will happen for you as well if you allow this revelation to become *your* revelation. That is why I wrote this book.

I will ask you the same question God asked me:

"Now who are you?"

2

MAN'S GREATEST NEED

GOD CREATED MAN as a being with needs. Outside the basic needs of physical survival such as food, water and shelter, we also have spiritual and emotional needs:

- to worship someone or something perceived as higher than ourselves
- to be loved
- companionship
- to reproduce
- to feel understood
- to be creative and productive

However, the greatest of these is the need to be loved. This need is so deep, that we will go to any length to satisfy it, whether in relationships, work, sports, hobbies, money, sex, material possessions, clothing style or being obsessed with our body and appearance. We can become man-pleasers, always concerned about how we are perceived by others. There is a drive within us that makes us feel that we must have something, be something, or do something to be noticed, loved and appreciated. Our society is filled with it. Advertising and marketing capitalize on this need within us. Songs have been written that are filled with these needs. TV shows, movies, books, magazines, billboards, signs, email and internet ads, all send messages to us dozens of times a day on how we can fulfill these needs. Buy this! Eat this! Wear this! Drive this! Take this! Go on this vacation! Smear this on! Live like this! They are constantly reminding us that we are missing something. The truth is we might be, but it is not found in the next purchase, the next accomplishment, the next job or next human relationship. Oh, we may find temporary pleasure and fulfillment from these things. But it doesn't last, it soon wears off. Why? Because we weren't created to fulfill our need for love through those things.

If this need to be loved is not fulfilled the way God intended, it can leave us feeling like something is missing, a chronic sense of anxiety and striving for the next conquest or accomplishment, false endeavors culminating in much worse conditions. It can lead directly into the darkness of depression and isolation where alleviation and comfort are often sought in more addictive behaviors like alcohol, drugs, homosexuality, pornography, sex change and even suicide. The need to be loved can easily be exploited by the devil.

The God who created every human being with the need to be loved also provided the way for this need to be met. It is met through Him simply by receiving His love — the unconditional love of the one true God as our Father.

It sounds so simple but receiving His love is difficult for many. John 3:16 says that God so loved the world that He gave His only begotten Son, that whoever puts their trust and faith in Him shall not perish but have eternal life. God already gave His love in the form of His Son Jesus. The problem is not in the giving but in the receiving.

Only when we receive the God of Love, as Father, into our hearts can we begin to heal and experience the abundant life as God intended.

> *Not that we are adequate in ourselves to consider anything as coming from ourselves, but our adequacy is from God.*
>
> 2 Corinthians 3:5

One of the truths of this scripture is that no man is sufficient unto himself. In other words, we don't have the internal resources to supply our own needs in such a way that we feel ultimate wholeness and peace. This is the reason why so many people are striving, looking for the next big thing—the next job, career, accomplishment, move, relationship...or even question their gender identity. They are always looking for that missing piece to bring fulfillment in their life. *If only I had this or were doing that.*

I will never forget a customer I had when I was just beginning my motorcycle shop. He called me to pick his bike up for repair from his house. He lived in a rich neighborhood. At that time, I had a baby blue 1968 Ford Van I purchased in an auction for $200. It was rusted so bad over the rear tires that when it snowed, the tires would throw snow inside the van and it would pile up. I pulled up into the big circular driveway in front of his mansion. He wasn't home yet so I waited, feeling desperately out of place in my van. Suddenly, here he came speeding up in his Porsche. We went inside and this house was amazing! Two kitchens! Huge living room with an all-glass wall on one side and a beautiful swimming pool just outside. He had several garages and one just for his motorcycle. As we were talking, he told me that he had worked very hard for his house and all his stuff. Then he said this: "And I have to work hard to keep it. My wife divorced me, my son is on drugs, and my daughter is a Dead Head (one who followed The Grateful Dead rock band)." He had the world's goods—success by man's measure—but lacked God's success.

It isn't much different with many Christians. We are just better at spiritualizing things and making our decisions sound godly. We go from one church to another, one job to another, move to a different house or even another state. We go from conference to conference, workshop to workshop, chasing certain speakers and ministers, looking for the next spiritual buzz, the next revelation, the missing key of understanding, physical healing, emotional healing, searching for that missing piece. We chase our definition of success to feel better about ourselves while missing the source of the core need.

This is understandable. We live in a dysfunctional world and many of us come from dysfunctional homes and grow up without proper validation, leaving us with an unhealthy self-image. Parents are human and most do the best they can in raising their children. God is the best parent anyone can have, and his first two children made a terrible decision, causing all of us heartache and Jesus to be crucified. We shouldn't blame God for their sinful choice. However, since many parents have come from dysfunctional homes as well, they too have poor self-images and self-worth. Consequently, this is often transferred to their children and the cycle continues. So, when we become followers of Christ, we enter our new life hindered, wounded and confused. Making matters worse, we have an enemy who wants to keep us that way and further our destruction.

Here is the good news. We can break this cycle! To begin, we must learn our true identity according to God's definition. We must learn that God the Father accepts us, loves us and validates us apart from what we do and even what we have done. We must learn that a profound change happens to us when we are born again. We are not the same as we once were. We may look the same, wear the same clothes, live in the same house, drive the same car and go to the same school or job, but we are not the same! This revelation is essential for all who are born again children of God. It is also critical for all who are called into ministry leadership, since we are called to lead others and exemplify Jesus.

> *Wounded people wound people.*

Not feeling validated and accepted creates a distorted self-image, low self-worth and feelings of insecurity which inevitably trigger a compulsive search for some kind of self-fulfillment. A person feeling these things may use anything or any person to build their worth in their own eyes. If you are a leader in the Body of Christ and have low self-worth, you could cause wounding in the hearts of those in your care. The consequences can be devastating to people and a ministry.

King Saul, the first king of Israel, is an example of a leader with low self-esteem and the effect it had on a nation. Simply stated: Wounded people wound people. In contrast, those who are whole and healthy are better equipped to help bring healing and wholeness to others.

The following list identifies some of the traits and tendencies of low self-worth. We all will experience some of these from time to time for short periods. However, if you are experiencing some of these on a regular basis, you may want to take a deeper look at the cause. The list is not exhaustive but serves as an example. This list is compiled from several resources as well as my own experience counseling others.

- Feelings of isolation and rejection
- Feelings of anger, suppressed loathing or rage
- Outbursts of anger
- Using anger to defend from getting hurt
- Difficulty getting along with others
- Overly sensitive; easily offended
- Less inclined to be transparent
- Lack of inner-peace
- Low self-confidence
- Feelings of jealousy, competition, and envy
- Inclined to be depressed and anxious
- Rejects compliments and expressions of love
- Feels they don't deserve to be loved
- A tendency to be a poor listener and a poor loser
- A tendency to withdraw socially, fears of being alone, fears of being with people
- Always has a better story than yours
- Needs external "things" to make them feel better
- A tendency to think God is angry and/or uninterested in them
- A tendency to be critical, legalistic, rigid and judgmental

- Strives to become "somebody", to be noticed
- A tendency to develop "clingy" type relationships (co-dependent)
- A tendency to sabotage relationships for fear of getting too close
- Over-commits easily
- A tendency to be either controlling and manipulative or overly submissive and yielding
- Struggles with authority
- Has boundary confusion with "black and white" thinking

A person struggling with any of the above issues feels rejected and insecure and will never be able to walk consistently in the promises and purposes of God. Therefore, having a healthy, biblical self-image is vital — it is a need that God created in us. How we view ourselves and the value we place on ourselves will shape our view of God, the world around us and the people in it.

Jesus was once asked to name the greatest commandment. Listen to His answer.

> *And He said to him, "You shall love the Lord your God with all your heart, and with all your soul, and with all your mind. This is the great and foremost commandment. The second is like it, you shall love your neighbor as yourself."*
> Matthew 22:37-39

We can read scriptures dozens of times, but it only takes that one time, when the Holy Spirit highlights something and the words leap off the page, to open our eyes to something we haven't seen before. I was reading

> *The traits we dislike in others are often the same ones we have ourselves but are too blind to see.*

this passage several years ago and the words caught my attention like never before. Jesus said the second commandment was like the first, that we should love our neighbor as our self. In other words, the amazing measuring stick of loving our neighbor is our own self-love! A healthy love of self is the necessary precondition to loving others. We may not realize it but how we view ourselves is superimposed onto others and our relationships. This understanding explains many of our relationship issues. It is interesting that the traits we dislike in others are often the same ones we have ourselves but are too blind to see.

> *For through the grace given to me I say to everyone among you not to think more highly of himself than he ought to think; but to think so as to have sound judgment, as God has allotted to each a measure of faith.*
>
> Romans 12:3

This verse tells us not to think more highly of ourselves than we ought. But notice that it does not forbid us thinking highly of ourselves, only thinking *more* highly than we should. There is a healthy balance.

The Lord does not instruct us to think poorly of our self, only to avoid thinking more highly than we ought. It is a common teaching in some Christian circles that we should see ourselves as some lowly, rotten, worthless, worm-like creature.

This is not how the Lord views us at all, neither before nor after we become His children by being born again. We need to have a balanced, scriptural perception of ourselves. Some falsely believe that thinking highly of themselves or loving themselves is pride. Sure, it is possible to go overboard and my ego be blown out of proportion. I can love myself so much that life becomes all about me. However, not thinking as highly as God does about ourselves is, in fact, a false, perverted humility, a deadly hidden pride that fails to accept oneself as God declares.

Here is the difference: We can never think too highly of ourselves as long as we see ourselves as we truly are: a part of the Creator and in a living relationship with Him. How can I think too highly of His creation? Of His handiwork? "I am fearfully and wonderfully made," (Psalm 139:14). It is when we view ourselves as our own work, apart from Creator God, that our view becomes pride. We can never think too highly with God. We are His. Anything less is false humility.

It is popular in Christian circles to say that we are "sinners saved by grace." In other words, to call ourselves sinners and say things like: "We are all sinners." This sounds humble but it is a partial truth. It is true that we are saved by grace but after we are born again, we are not called sinners in scripture. It may be surprising to learn that nowhere in scripture does God say that His children are "sinners saved by grace." You can't find it in the New Testament except in the case of one who falls away from God and reverts to a lifestyle prior to his born-again experience.

> *My brethren, if any among you strays from the truth and one turns him back, let him know that he who turns a sinner from the error of his way will save his soul from death and will cover a multitude of sins"*
>
> James 5:19-20

We may still sin but that doesn't make us sinners. I can bark but that doesn't make me a dog. I love to swim but that doesn't make me a fish.

To call someone a sinner is to describe a person's state of being, their nature, their identity. The difference is this: A sinner lives a lifestyle of sin. It is their way of life even though they may do acts of righteousness at times.

> *A sinner lives a lifestyle of sin. It is their way of life even though they may do acts of righteousness at times.*

True children of God love and practice a lifestyle of righteousness even though they may sin at times. This transformation is only possible because our identity has changed. We have received a new Christ-like nature and the love of God has been shed abroad in our heart. The basic source of our behavior, whether sinful or righteous, flows out of our perception of God and ourselves. What we believe about ourselves is what we tend to become. If we believe we are sinners or failures, our incorrect thoughts construct a false identification and affect the way we speak and behave.

The reverse is also true. If we believe the truth about ourselves, based on what God says about us, that will also affect the way we speak, how we behave and the direction of our lives. It is the natural outcome of our perceived identity. Proverbs 23:7 says: For as he [a man] thinks within himself, so he is. What we think about ourselves is what we tend to become.

> *We behold what we identify with and we become what we behold.*

For instance, if I believe I am a sinner, not only do I have an excuse for sinning, but I also believe that sinning is a part of my identity and therefore my life. It becomes an assumed result. This false belief will keep me trapped in a false identity. 2 Corinthians 5:17 says that the moment we are born again, we are new creatures, new creations, and that old things have passed away as new things have come. Many Christians believe they are sinners due to an incorrect belief system and bad teaching. The truth rests with God—the way He views us and what He says about us. The truth does not rest upon what we have been taught or have always believed.

Consider this: We behold what we identify with and we become what we behold. To behold means to fix our attention on, to reflect upon and compare to. Have you ever been driving your car down a road and begin to look at something on either side of the road? Suddenly your car begins drifting in that direction. That is because our focus is in that direction, causing us to move that way. When we focus on sin and failure, we begin going in that direction and experiencing the negative consequences of it. Yet when we shift our focus to behold Jesus, we become more like Him.

> *But we all, with unveiled face, beholding as in a mirror the glory of the Lord, are being transformed into the same image from glory to glory, just as from the Lord, the Spirit.*
>
> 2 Corinthians 3:18

Another example is the belief in evolution. Believing in evolution shapes our thoughts and belief system regarding our origin as humans. How does that affect our view of our identity, purpose and destiny? When we sift through the layers of the evolutionary process, we eventually come to the logical conclusion that our identity is founded on an animal, and eventually, on a protoplasmic mass. If we believe we came from an animal and we identify with them, at least to some degree, then it will be both permissible and even appropriate to act like one because that is what we assume we are.

Our thoughts have determined our belief and our beliefs have determined our outcome. Animals live only by instincts, drives, and appetites aimed at self-preservation, protection and procreation. It would then be ok to live by my own desires, which many people do. God has created us humans for much more than this!

This is just one small example of how dangerous it can be to believe a lie about our identity. Believing the truth of who we are and what we are will help us to determine our purpose and our destiny. The Bible tells us to retrain the way we think by renewing our minds (ref. Romans 12:2). We align our thinking with God's thinking. We get into the scripture allowing the Holy Spirit to reveal the truth of our identity. Then we feed on that truth and choose to believe what God says, period. We will discuss this more in a later chapter.

Our thoughts determine what we believe. What we believe determines our words and actions. To change our actions, we must begin by changing the way we think. Typically, we end up at wrong conclusions when we begin at the wrong starting place. We must begin with God and what He says, or we will arrive at an incorrect conclusion.

Sometimes our relationships, jobs or the activities we engage in slowly begin to form our identity. As I mentioned in chapter one, before I changed my occupation, I owned a motorcycle parts and repair shop. I identified myself much of the time as a motorcycle mechanic and business owner. I believed that this was my identity and I didn't realize that was happening at the time. Of course, I knew I was a child of God, but that became secondary. It was just part of who I was and not the substance of who or what I was. I took pride in being a motorcycle mechanic and a business owner. Over time, I found that I received most of my significance or value from these titles and activities. My identity came to be based on my performance — what I did and what I owned — not on who I truly am. As long as I performed up to my standards and made profits, my self-worth was inflated. But if the opposite happened, I was deflated and felt devalued. Therefore, how I felt about

> *Our thoughts determine what we believe. What we believe determines our words and actions. To change our actions, we must begin by changing the way we think.*

myself was directly linked to my occupation, performance, circumstances and others' reactions. As I look back now, I realize my identity began to be defined by my job title and job performance rather than by God's word. The shift was very subtle and slow, but nevertheless continued to occur, and I didn't realize it was happening. I have found that this is a typical pattern of behavior for many people and especially men. It is characteristic of our world's system.

Today, as I lead a congregation, I see the same thing happening to some pastors and ministry leaders. It is easy for some pastors to feel like a failure when they do not have a certain number of people in their congregation. Why? Because in the church world we have mis-defined success and what it means to produce fruit. Success to many pastors is attaining to some mystical number in their congregation or Sunday morning worship attendance. Too often success is based on how well a meeting, class or event was attended. Whether it be 100, 300, 1,000 or more, when that number isn't met, they may feel a sense of failure and inadequacy compared to their peers. There is only one way God determines success; faithfulness. And faithfulness produces fruitfulness.

How often have we gained our definition of our identity from our occupation, title, position or performance instead of God's definition? How do we finally come to realize we are valuable simply because we exist as God's wonderful creation? If we belong to God, He will pose the question of identity upon us by pulling out the props, exposing the very things, people and circumstances that gave meaning to our lives in this way. He will compel us to dig deep and discover what He thinks of us and what we think of ourselves. It may be painful, no, it will hurt, but go there. The end result is so worth it!

He is restoring the breach between Himself as Father and His children. As a result, healing between fathers and their children will occur.

> *"Behold, I am going to send you Elijah the prophet before the coming of the great and terrible day of the Lord. He will restore the hearts of the fathers to their children and the hearts of the children to their fathers, so that I will not come and smite the land with a curse."*
> Malachi 4:5-6

As important as the healing of relationships between parents and children is, the ultimate purpose of this prophetic restoration is to reconnect our hearts to the heart of God as our Father. The fact that He planned this restoration process over 3,000 years ago reflects His loving heart as our Father. We must get to know God as our loving Father and even more intimately, as Abba, Daddy, Papa or whatever word is intimate and personal between you and Him. Only when our hearts are healed and whole, do we enjoy the abundant life that Jesus came to give us and the peace and rest we were created for. As we come to understand and receive revelation about our identity, it will propel us to fulfill our God-given destiny on earth. We will then be free to function in our calling to full potential with all the gifts, talents and abilities He has given us.

Genetically, we know it is the DNA (or seed) of our biological fathers, conveyed through sperm, that determines our gender. So, whether we have ever met them or not, or whether we like it or not, we inherit specific biological traits from our fathers. We also receive other seeds of identity from our fathers (as well as our mothers) by simply watching them and learning to do what they do. How a father treats people or interacts in business situations, for example, can be behavior that is learned by a child. If we did not grow up with a father, we receive these seeds from our mothers or another father-figure in our lives.

When I grew up at home, my dad was meticulous about yard work and keeping the house, garage and basement cleaned and organized. I was made to work on a regular basis as a child and I hated it. But now, as an adult, I have a work ethic that I am very glad was imparted to me. I now love yard work and I keep my home clean and organized (well, mostly organized) and I actually enjoy it. When my father wasn't in my life during some of my teenage years, my grandfather, my brother-in-law and an uncle imparted things to me that have stuck with me into my adult years.

In our North American culture, children typically receive their father's last name, which gives us further identification. And not too long ago, a child from unmarried parents who had no father's last name on his birth certificate was looked down on as illegitimate.

There has been much debate on the definition of marriage in recent years. The Supreme Court of the United States has determined that same-sex marriage is legal under the Constitution. But just because it is legal in our nation doesn't make it legal in the Kingdom in which we live as God's children. God created marriage to be between one biological man and one biological woman. Marriage is an illustration of our relationship and union with the Lord. Only a man and a woman can procreate, thereby fulfilling the mandate of God by being fruitful and multiplying. Having parents that are either lesbians (two mothers) or homosexuals (two fathers) perverts the created order and gives a child a warped sense of who God is. When the identity or image of God is distorted, then so will our identity be distorted as a being created in the image of God and according to His likeness. We can easily see how the devil is working hard today to distort the image of God and pervert our identity.

These are just some examples of how our identity, and therefore our values, are shaped as we grow from childhood to adulthood.

The love we receive from our fathers helps establish our self-worth. It is generally understood that the way we interact with our earthly father and perceive the love he gives or withholds forms our earliest and most lasting concepts of God. Negative impressions can be overcome in the Lord, however. God created us with the need to be loved, and out of that love comes all the building blocks of identity: acceptance, affection, value, security, comfort, self-worth and self-esteem. If that love is missing or abused, a child suffers. The profile of many prisoners reveals that the lack of a stable father consistently leads to serious problems. This is one of the reasons that Satan has attacked the family, and especially the role of the father, so severely. Our father is the first example we have of God.

For many people, the thought of God being a father is unattractive, even repulsive. They have had earthly fathers who were abusive sexually, physically, or emotionally. Their fathers may have even abandoned them and their mothers. Other people were perhaps neglected and have never known their fathers intimately or at all. Those who have not had overt abuse or neglect still find themselves wounded in certain areas of their lives. Obviously, because we are sinful, imperfect beings, not many of us had all the love we wanted or even needed growing up. So those emotional wounds create a void in our hearts that need healing. Thankfully, that healing is available for us at whatever level of loss we have experienced. It is found in a loving relationship with our Heavenly Father.

Healing is available for us at whatever level of loss we have experienced.

The Bible says that God is love. "The one who does not love does not know God, for God is love" (1 John 4:8). Love gives, and because God is love, He gave Himself to us. Even when we were His enemies, He loved us and gave to us in order to redeem us out of the desperate situation we were in. God doesn't just tell us He loves us, He demonstrates it. His love has actions that prove it. Think of it this way. Since God is love, until we receive Him, we haven't experienced the true, unconditional love we were created for. There are many Scripture passages which illustrate this point. I will just mention two.

> *For God so loved the world, that He gave His only begotten Son, that whoever believes in Him should not perish, but have eternal life. For God did not send the Son into the world to judge the world, but that the world should be saved through Him.*
>
> John 3:16-17

> *But God demonstrates His own love toward us, in that while we were yet sinners, Christ died for us.*
>
> Romans 5:8

Love is not merely a feeling; it is a decision that requires action whether we feel anything or not. When we receive the unconditional love of God however, we will experience emotions as a result. Father God loves us so much that He gave Jesus to us so that we would be re-established in an intimate relationship of love with Him. Even if you did not have a loving relationship with your biological father or any other father figure in your life, you can experience the unconditional love of your Father in Heaven. And by learning the truth of your new identity in Him, the love of God will grow even deeper.

Father God is our greatest need because He is Love and love is our greatest need. Love is the most powerful force on the planet. Love can penetrate the hardest of hearts. Love sets us free and heals our hearts. God created us with that need so nothing or no one else could satisfy it but Him. Receiving His unconditional love sets us free and heals our hearts. It gives us value, worth, acceptance and significance. It is the fuel and power for life.

> [God's] *Love never fails.*
>
> 1 Corinthians 13:8 (emphasis added)

But now faith, hope, love, abide, these three; but the greatest of these is love.

           1 Corinthians 13:13

3

WHAT IS MAN?

What is man that You take thought of him, and the son of man that You care for him?

Psalm 8:4

IN THE BEGINNING, everything that God created besides man was spoken into existence using the third person, which reflected God's separation and distinctness from the created order. He said, "Let there be... (light, sky, water, stars, plants and animals)" and there was. The creation account is also careful to describe everything that God created as being brought forth "after their (or its) kind." However, when God created man, the language shifts from third person to first person. "Let Us make man in Our image, according to Our likeness," (Genesis 1:26). This implies personal attention and intimacy.

God used the words, "in Our image, according to Our likeness" instead of "after their kind" as He did when creating the other living beings. Genesis 2:7 says, "Then the Lord God formed man of dust from the ground and breathed into his nostrils the breath of life; and man became a living being." God was hands-on when making and fashioning man. He breathed His own breath of life into man. Think of it: All that is on the inside of God the Father was breathed into man. God breathed His Spirit, nature and life into man, and man became a living being! Wow! His very breath became our breath that brought us life! In just these two images alone, the Lord shows us that from the very beginning, man was completely different and more superior to any other created being. Man was created for relationship. He alone was set apart and blessed with an intimacy not experienced by another creature.

Man is not merely different from any other created being; he is also like his Creator. To be made in His own image, as God said: "Let Us make man in Our image, according to Our likeness" (Genesis 1:27), is to be a representation of the Father, a copy or counterpart that reflects His original likeness. The Hebrew word *selem*, which means "image" in this passage, also means a model or statue, even an idol. "According to Our likeness" suggests a concrete model or resemblance of Him. The word *demût*, which means likeness in this passage, means a pattern, shape and form taken directly from the original.

Jesus illustrated this point in Matthew 22:19-21 when He was questioned about paying the poll-tax.

> *"Show Me the coin used for the poll-tax."* And *they brought Him a denarius. And He said to them, "Whose likeness* (eikon) *and inscription is this?" They said to Him, "Caesar's." Then He said to them, "Then render to Caesar the things that are Caesar's; and to God the things that are God's."*
>
> Matthew 22:19-21 (parenthesis added)

An *eikon* is an image or sign that by its very form suggests its meaning. The image or *eikon* that was imprinted on the coin was that of Caesar. God obviously doesn't have a coin. He has us, humanity, and His image is imprinted on us. The Pharisees knew the creation account of Genesis 1 and how man is made in God's image. What bears His image belongs to Him. So, man is the only created being to model God in form as well as function. Think about that!

No other creature was made this way except man. We see similar language used of Jesus in Colossians 1:15 where Jesus is said to be in "the image of God" and "the firstborn of all creation." Interestingly, the same Greek word *eikon* is used in both the Genesis and the Colossians passages. This Greek word, *eikon*, is where we get the word *icon* or *image*, which we know is an exact replica of the thing it represents. Jesus is the *eikon* of God and so is man—you and I. Hmm..., when we learn that we are made in God, the Creator of the universe's image, it adds to our understanding of the high place we have in His eyes compared to the rest of creation.

Through Adam, God gave man the task of naming, literally proclaiming, a name over every creature that He created. Adam looked over every insect and bug, every four-footed beast, every bird of the air and every fish of the sea and decreed their name. He not only determined their name, but he gave them names that explained their characteristics, material essence and reality. We don't recognize this in the English language, but it is apparent in Hebrew. One by one, God presented these creatures to man to see what he would call them. By this act of naming, several lessons were being taught.

First, God was showing Adam that the whole created order was under his (Adam's) authority.

Second, as God's image-bearing representative, Adam was also being taught that nothing bore his (Adam's) image. He was like his Creator in nature, but God had no flesh or bones. He was distinct from everything else in the created realm. He was alone in that sense. And so, we learn that it was immediately after the naming project that Adam came face to face with the fact that there was no creature like him. The animals came two by two, but there was no counterpart to himself, nothing that bore his image.

It is not good for man to be living as one or in solitude.

Just prior to Adam naming all the animals, God said it is not good for mankind to be alone. This is the first thing He said that was *not good* for mankind. Let's not miss the point. He didn't say that it wasn't good for man to be unmarried. (Although, it is definitely not good for some men and women to be unmarried, for their sakes and for the continuation of the human race.) No, God said *alone*, which literally means that it is not good for man to be living as one or in solitude. In other words, it is not good for man to be isolated.

In response to His own pronouncement, God caused a deep sleep to fall upon Adam (ref. Genesis 2:21-22). As he slept, God took one of his ribs. The word *rib* is translated from the Hebrew word, *tsalah*, which means "a side." God took a whole lot more from man than a rib! Literally, God took one side of man. He didn't just take a rib bone from Adam and fashion Eve out of it. He actually took a side of Adam (or mankind) and fashioned the woman. Man is one side of humankind and Woman is one side of humankind. Then God brought the woman to the man and the man said,

> *"This is now bone of my bones,*
> *And flesh of my flesh;*
> *She shall be called Woman* (ishah)*,*
> *Because she was taken out of Man* (ish)*"*
> Genesis 2:23 (parenthesis added)

This describes the intimacy between man and woman as equals before God. Woman is not a mere extension of man as an inferior being. She is an individual with equality, standing side by side with the man. Since her body is made from man's, she is a perfect counterpart to him and he to her. Only in this way: one biological man and one biological woman, can they be "one flesh." This is revealed perfectly in the Hebrew text where Adam, who is called *ish* (or man) immediately names Eve *ishah* (or woman) realizing that she is a part of him—one side of him. So along with the name, Adam also recognized that there was now one found suitable for him.

Interestingly, within the Hebrew word for man and woman, *ish* (אִישׁ) and *ishah* (אִשָּׁה), there is one letter in *ish* (man) that is not in *ishah* (woman), the letter *yod*, י. There is also one letter in *ishah* (woman) that is not in *ish* (man), the letter *hey*, ה. *Yod* (י) and *hey* (ה) form the basis for the name YHWH, יהוה, the Hebrew name for God that is mentioned in scripture thousands of times. Hebrew is read from right to left. So, man and woman together give a more complete picture of who God is. YHWH, יהוה, infused us with His DNA.

Even today, we have the privilege of naming things that we have authority over, that belong to us or that we are in relationship with: e.g., our country and cities, our inventions and ideas, our pets and most importantly, our children.

Among other things, it is clear that we, like Adam, need to be reminded of how distinct we are from all of God's creation and how much we are like God Himself. This is one of many reasons why the Theory of Evolution and other ideas are so detrimental to our self-image and our self-worth. We, unlike animals or protoplasm, are like God and created in His image.

Psalm 8:4 asks, "What is man that you take thought of him?" I believe this is a question many ask, and it is one we need to find the answer to. But not just any answer, we need to find God's answer. The Bible says we are God's handcrafted creation with which He exercised special care and detail. We share God's nature and identity, and He has given us the capacity to demonstrate His character traits and contain His Spirit. We are the only beings that were created for the purpose of intimate communion with God on the deepest possible level— spirit to Spirit.

Man truly is made in the image of God and according to His likeness. God has dominion of the heavens, but man was given dominion and rule over every other created thing. Psalm 115:16 says, "The heavens are the heavens of the LORD, but the earth He has given to the sons of men." What an amazing God and Father we have, one who not only shares His dominion and kingdom but most of all, His own image with man. When we are born again, we become one of God's children, alike in nature. Even the three parts of man: spirit, soul and body, are reflected from the Triune God: Father, Son and Holy Spirit. God the Father is reflected by our soul—our mind, will and emotions. The Holy Spirit is reflected by our spirit, for He is Spirit. And Jesus, having a body of flesh, is reflected in our body. All three in perfect harmony and unity.

Think of this declaration the Apostle Paul makes to the Ephesians when he acknowledges that the whole family derives its name from God.

> *For this reason I bow my knees before the Father, from whom every (whole) family (lineage) in heaven and on earth derives its name.*
> Ephesians 3:14-15 (parenthesis added)

When we belong to God's family, we inherit a name that is eternal, majestic, and holy.

4

IDENTIFICATION

I·den·ti·fi·ca·tion, (ī͵den tə fə'kā shen) – A process whereby an individual relates to a person or group with feelings of close emotional association.

I LOVE FOOTBALL and when I was younger, I enjoyed playing it. Living in New York for a time, the New York Jets were my favorite team. My hero was number 12, Joe Namath, the Jets' quarterback. My Dad and I never missed a game when they were on TV. He took me to see the Jets play at Shea Stadium on occasion. I even had a Jets helmet and a Joe Namath jersey. Life was good!

Later, as I journeyed through my tumultuous teen years, I identified with rock music. I was not a musician but loved music, attended many concerts and owned dozens of records and eight tracks (anyone remember those?). To identify with my idols, I grew my hair long and dressed in jeans and black t-shirts. I owned lots of black t-shirts. I was unaware of what I was doing, but like so many young people, I was searching for identity, an association by which to pattern myself. I was looking to belong.

Every person identifies with something or someone, to see ourselves as closely related or identical. There are many ways we identify ourselves: by gender, family name, ethnicity, occupation, sports, school, music, talents, politics, clothes, money, religion and many other ways.

One of our first associations is with our family. When we are asked by someone who we are, we typically answer with our name. I would answer, "Joe Nicola." In most families, our first name is unique and our last name, which comes from our father is shared among family members. Sometimes we are identified by our last name only; that identifies us with a particular family group as well as being more unique than a first name. When I was in the military, I was called by my last name the majority of the time. Another way we identify ourselves is by our occupation. Earlier in my life, I would say I was a motorcycle mechanic. Then later I would say I am a youth pastor. Now I typically say I am a son of God. Notice how we usually say, "I am" *this* or *that*. When we say, "I am", we are making a statement that identifies us.

It is interesting how we automatically identify certain people when we hear their name. For instance; if I said "Elvis," what would come to mind? We probably would think of Elvis Presley and would say he was a great entertainer, singer, musician or maybe an actor (for those of us who remember *Jail House Rock*).

How about the name George Washington? I think of a great leader, general and the first president of the United States. When you hear the name Tiger Woods or John Wayne, what do you associate their names with? Tiger Woods is a championship golfer and John Wayne was a movie star.

Identification

See what I mean? We associate people with something they are known for. There are many people in different realms of society we remember in this way. This is natural and normal. It is also interesting that typically we associate people's names with something they do or have accomplished, not necessarily for who they are as an individual person. One reason for this is that we really do not know famous people. We only know them for what they are known for.

Obviously, everyone has a mother and a father even if they never knew one or both parents. Our mothers and fathers have certain ethnic genes that are passed along to us. In my case, my father is Lebanese and my mother has an ethnic mix. So, I have more Lebanese in me than the other ethnicities my mother has. Many people, even children of God, identify with their ethnicity more than their new identity in Christ. They associate more with being Caucasian, African American, Asian, Chinese, Native American or Hispanic, etc., than they do with being God's son or daughter.

As a note; I resist using the word "race" to differentiate between ethnicities because scientists have concluded that all humans belong to one race, the human race. Therefore, it is incorrect to delineate the different ethnicities as separate races even though it is very common to do so. Regardless of the color of our skin, the origin of our birth, rich or poor, or whether we have disabilities, every human being has been created in the image of God according to His likeness. Therefore, every human being has value and worth! If we constantly focus on our differences, we will always see ourselves as different and separate from others. This does not create unity but disunity. It also leads to thinking we are better than some and worse than others. How often did Jesus identify Himself as a Jew? Not once! Jesus never identified Himself by His natural ethnicity. His identity was tied to His Father, not to His earthly stepfather Joseph. Jesus never self-identified with being a step son. I am not saying we should ignore our ethnicity or ignore our family heritage. Rather, as followers of Christ, we are exhorted in scripture not to recognize one another by the flesh (natural) any longer. This would also include ourselves.

> *Therefore from now on we recognize no one according to the flesh* (natural)*; even though we have known Christ according to the flesh* (natural)*, yet now we know Him in this way no longer.*
> 2 Corinthians 5:16 (parenthesis added)

A major area of identification for many Christians is with Adam. The name Adam means man or mankind, which is fitting since he was the first human created by God. Adam and his wife, Eve, disobeyed God by eating from the Tree of the Knowledge of Good and Evil. God told Adam beforehand that if he ate from that tree, he would surely die. Death is a perversion of life, a corruption of God's creation. Because of their disobedience, a curse was released that caused this corruption called death that affects all of God's creation on earth. The curse of death is now an existence separated from the life of God (*zoe* is the Greek word meaning the life of God. It is the same quality of life that Jesus experienced). Jesus referred to this as the abundant life

Identification

(zoe) in John 10:10. Therefore, all men must be born from above (born again) to escape this curse of death and receive the zoe, life of God. This gives us a new identity recreated in God's image.

We associate Adam with a fallen, sinful nature. We tend to identify with sin and disobedience—conditions we associate with Adam—more than we do with the righteousness and wholeness that our new Christ-like nature represents. This is because of some popular teachings in the Body of Christ that have led us to develop an incorrect belief system, making us more sin conscious than God or righteousness conscious. The new birth in Christ severs us from the grip that the corruption of this world has on us and restores to us the life of God! This is a very powerful effect that the new birth in Christ has on us when we understand it, renew our mind and begin to walk in its truth and reality. 2 Peter 1:4 tells us that we partake of the divine nature, escaping the corruption that is in the world. Wow!

> *For by these He has granted to us His precious and magnificent promises, so that by them you may become partakers of the divine nature, having escaped the corruption that is in the world by lust.*
>
> 2 Peter 1:4

The story of the Prodigal Son can be found in Luke 15:11-32. There are three main characters in this story—a father and his two sons. The younger son asks his father for his share of the inheritance. When the father gives the younger son his share, he also gives the older son his share. Even though the younger son asked for it, the father gave it to both. Not only did the older son get his share of the inheritance, but as a Jew, he would have received a double portion. Sometime after receiving his inheritance, the younger son leaves and wastes all his inheritance on riotous living. He is now broke and starving. He finds work by feeding pigs where he longs to eat the pods he is feeding to them.

When he comes to himself, he says, "I will return to my father." He gets up and returns to his father. His father welcomes him back home and puts a robe on his back, a ring on his finger and sandals on his feet. His father restores him to his rightful place, promotes him, then throws a party for him to celebrate.

When God restores, He doesn't just place us where we were. He promotes us beyond where we were!

When God restores, He doesn't just place us where we were. He promotes us beyond where we were!

Notice that since the younger son asked for his inheritance, he knew that one belonged to him because he understood he was a son and not a slave. Slaves don't ask for an inheritance because they know that one doesn't belong to them. Notice the words he used after he had spent all he had and finally came to himself, he said; "I will get up and go to my father." He didn't say, "I will return home." There is a difference between returning to a place and returning to a person. He knew who his father was, and it was to his father that he returned. He had an understanding of son-ship and his home was wherever his father was.

Identification

When the younger son returned, his father gave him a party while the older son was in the field working. As the older son approached the house, he heard music and dancing. Notice where the older son was. He was in the field working with the slaves. He was not in the house with the family. His brother had come home. Preparations for a celebration had taken place, and the party had started. But the older son didn't have any idea what was going on. He was so disconnected from his father he had to ask a slave what was happening in his own house.

He became angry when he learned that his father welcomed his brother back and was throwing a party for him. As a result, he spoke with blatant disrespect to his father. Pay close attention to the words he uses and the words he doesn't use. He never calls his father, "father," and he only refers to his brother as "this son of yours." He was mad at his father for not ever throwing him a party with his friends. It is interesting how little he knew his own father. It seems his father's answer was a surprise to him. His father told him he could have had a party any time he wanted because everything the father had also belonged to him as His son.

Because the older son never used family terms such as father or brother, we see that he really had an orphan spirit resulting in a slave mentality. He didn't have much of a relationship with his father or his brother. It was more of a business or contractual relationship. The older son believed he had earned the right to a party with a fattened calf. He was given his share of the inheritance, which, as I already mentioned, would have been twice as much as the younger son had received. But he never took advantage of it. He didn't even mention it! The younger son had more of a son mentality, even though he had left his father. He knew who he was as a son, who his father was and what belonged to him. When he was in trouble he knew where to go and to whom to return. The older son never understood that.

In the family of God, we are either a son with a son mentality or a son with a slave mentality. The way we relate to God the Father and others around us is determined by which of these mindsets we have. Both sons and slaves have similar functions. Both serve. However, only sons inherit. Sons serve out of love for their Father because they have received love from their Father. Slaves serve out of obligation, legalism, guilt, shame, fear, striving to earn God's favor or love, etc. Slaves do not have a Father son (child) relationship with God. The slave mentality prevents them from this.

> *No longer do I call you slaves, for the slave does not know what his master is doing; but I have called you friends, for all things that I have heard from My Father I have made known to you.*
> John 15:15

If we have a slave mentality, it will keep us from accessing all the resources of the Kingdom of Heaven. As sons of God, we have authority to rule and reign over the earth in this life. If we do not realize this truth, we will not exercise the authority God has delegated to us as His sons.

It may help to look at it from the perspectives of a business owner versus an employee. Both owner and employee work. However, the owner is obviously the one

Identification

who owns everything. It is all his, so he takes ownership and responsibility for it. He knows it all belongs to him and he oversees it all like a good steward. No one works as hard as an owner. I found that out firsthand.

An employee, on the other hand, is not an owner but a hired hand. A typical employee does what it takes to get by. He works for payday, the benefits and the weekend. An employee knows he does not have much authority.

We are the ones who determine which mentality we will develop—a son/owner or a slave/employee in God's house. The mentality we have will make all the difference in how we see ourselves, how we function within God's family, how we pray, the authority we walk in, and whether or not we fulfill our destiny.

Do you have a slave/employee mentality or a son/owner mentality? Here are some characteristics of each. Read over this list carefully.

Sons build; they volunteer and work hard. They initiate and go the extra mile.

Slaves are not initiators. They just do the bare minimum to get by. They will not go the extra mile. They use words like, "I'm not called to that." They expect something in return for their service and have an entitlement mentality.

Sons regard the father's heart and his success as their own. "If you are not faithful with that which is another man's, who will give you your own?" (Luke 16:12). Sons know they have an inheritance.

Slaves look out for their own interests and success. Slaves don't wait to inherit their ministry; they go out and try to make it happen.

Sons are always family oriented. Family relationships come first. When making decisions and setting priorities, they ask themselves, "How does this affect my family?" Family relationships come before doing ministry.

Slaves are issue and program oriented. They feel they have to do ministry and are concerned with issues. They will split the family over an issue. They think in terms of their rights and desires.

Sons use the language of family: we, our, us. They believe that another's problem is their problem. If the family is under attack, they are under attack, and they respond accordingly. It is personal with them.

Slaves use individual terminology. They say I, me, them and they. They have a "Your problem is your problem" attitude. They say things like, "They won't allow me to do this or that." They have an "us" versus "them" perspective.

Sons honor authority. They cover their father's nakedness (ref. Genesis 9:23). When one in authority makes a mistake, they cover them.

Slaves expose their father's nakedness, mistakes and sins to exalt themselves and gain an advantage.

Sons honor naturally the chain of command. They understand that Jesus operates through delegated authority.

Identification

Slaves continually question those in authority over them. They usually will not submit to any authority figure who they don't like or don't agree with.

Sons want to share their lives with the father's life and will give themselves to accomplish His will. They assume the Father's agenda.

Slaves have their own agenda. They hide, misrepresent and manipulate.

Sons bond people to the father and the family.

Slaves bond people to themselves.

Sons are focused on the welfare of the people. They feel secure in the Father's love. They are concerned with pleasing the Lord and accomplishing His will.

Slaves are focused on appearance. How does what we do or are involved in look to others? They are people pleasers for personal benefit. They get their esteem from what they do and what people think of them not from who they are.

Sons share their inner conversations. They will tell you what they really think and feel, not what they think you want to hear.

Slaves will tell you only what they think you want to hear to try and impress or give a false impression.

Sons can handle discipline, correction and change. They will take the blame if they've done wrong.

Slaves see discipline as rejection and won't receive it. They tend to blame someone or something else. They are easily offended.

Sons are teachable. They are willing to learn and aren't afraid of making mistakes in the process. Excellence is a priority.

Slaves are not teachable. They are afraid of making mistakes and they want to teach you.

When one is born again, an actual material change occurs. We receive a new identity with which we should begin to associate. We are not who we used to be.

> *Therefore if anyone is in Christ, he is a new creature; the old things passed away; behold, new things have come.*
>
> 2 Corinthians 5:17

Take a moment and consider how you identify yourself. Do you identify mainly by your ethnicity, with Adam and sin, as a slave, your occupation, or some way other than who God says you are? When you pray, do you ask God for things He has already given you? Or do you ask Him to do things He has told you to do? Praying like this may be a result of ignorance or it may be because of a wrong mindset, a slave mentality.

The day I was kicked out of high school, a friend and I had our ears pierced. I wore an earring in my left ear for some time. When I received Christ, I removed it. The earring was a sign of my rebellion and I didn't want anything to do with it. About seven years later I woke up one Sunday morning in the Fall of 1990 and the Holy Spirit spoke to me and said, "Put your earring in."

Huh?! Put my earring in? I thought to myself, I don't even have an earring. I dug through my wife's jewelry box and found a gold stud and to my amazement, it went

Identification

through the hole in my ear. I wasn't sure why the Lord would tell me to do this until sometime later I came across this scripture:

> *If you buy a Hebrew slave, he shall serve for six years; but on the seventh he shall go out as a free man without payment. If he comes alone, he shall go out alone; if he is the husband of a wife, then his wife shall go out with him. If his master gives him a wife, and she bears him sons or daughters, the wife and her children shall belong to her master, and he shall go out alone. But if the slave plainly says, 'I love my master, my wife and my children; I will not go out as a free man,' then his master shall bring him to God, then he shall bring him to the door or the doorpost. And his master shall pierce his ear with an awl; and he shall serve him permanently.*
>
> Exodus 21:2-6

It was then that I learned the difference between a slave and a bond-slave. A bond-slave is a slave by choice. Sons are free, but by their own volition they choose to serve their Father.

If you have received Christ and been born again, *choose* to be a son, *think* like a son and *act* like a son. Because that is who you are!

5

THE MAN JESUS

Image: (Greek word eikon, English word icon), "the very substance or essential embodiment of something or someone."

TO HELP US UNDERSTAND our new identity when we are born again, we must first understand who Jesus is and how He lived on the earth. We will only understand who and what we are in light of who Jesus truly is and how He lived. Specifically, did Jesus live as God or did He live as man? Did Jesus preach, perform miracles and die on the cross as God? Or did He do all those things as a man empowered by God? These are very important questions that we must clearly understand if we are going to understand our own identity. Let's consider the following scriptures.

> *By this you know the Spirit of God: every spirit that confesses that Jesus Christ has come in the flesh is from God; and every spirit that does not confess Jesus is not from God; and this is the spirit of the antichrist, of which you have heard that it is coming, and now it is already in the world.*
>
> 1 John 4:2-3

> *For many deceivers have gone out into the world, those who do not acknowledge Jesus Christ as coming in the flesh. This is the deceiver and the antichrist.*
>
> 2 John 1:7

According to these passages, it is possible to know the difference between the Spirit of God and the antichrist spirit (the spirit that is not from God). Continuing from 1 John 4 verse 6, "By this we know the spirit of truth and the spirit of error." How are we going to know the difference? The answer is above in verses 2 and 3: "every spirit that confesses that Jesus came in the flesh is from God; and every spirit that does not confess Jesus is not from God." It is important to understand the phrase "confesses that Jesus came in the flesh."

Every major religion believes that Jesus was a man who lived on earth. There is too much historical proof to believe otherwise. The issue, however, is who they believe He was. Some will say He was a good man, and others even say He was a prophet. However, not all believe He was the Messiah, Son of the living God. Heck, not even the Jewish leaders believed it when Jesus was standing right in front of them! Then there are different beliefs within the Christian community. Many Christians believe Jesus was actually God in the flesh. Some say Jesus was fully God and fully man at the same time. Others have no idea how to answer.

Therefore, for someone to confess that Jesus came in the flesh as a man on earth cannot be enough to distinguish between truth and error. However, there is more to the phrase, "Jesus came in the flesh," than just believing that Jesus was a man. The word "flesh" means to be human with all of the limitations and weaknesses that are associated with being human. Which means Jesus was susceptible to all the same challenges, temptations, confusion, loss, fears, inadequacies, cuts, bruises, hunger, tiredness, sickness, diseases, etc. as we are. 1 John 4:17 says, "As He is, so also are we in this world." In other words, Jesus came to earth fully human with all human weaknesses and limitations just as we are, even though He is the Son of God. And, just like us, He was completely dependent upon God for everything. Philippians explains it this way;

> *Have this attitude in yourselves which was also in Christ Jesus, who, although He existed in the form of God, did not regard equality with God a thing to be grasped, but emptied Himself, taking the form of a bond-servant, and being made in the likeness of men. And being found in appearance as a man, He humbled Himself by becoming obedient to the point of death, even death on a cross.*
>
> Philippians 2:5-8

Jesus willingly laid aside His privileges and power as Deity to become a man limited by human weakness, dependent on His Father. It was required that Jesus come to earth as a man since God gave delegated authority over the earth to man (ref. Genesis 1:28, Psalms 115:16). Jesus could not even command angels directly. He needed to ask His Father. "Or do you think that I cannot appeal to

My Father, and He will at once put at My disposal more than twelve legions of angels?" (Matthew 26:53).

Everything Jesus did, whether miraculous or not, was done as a man filled with the Holy Spirit in complete obedience to His Father. He laid aside the voluntary exercise of His divine attributes: omnipotence, omniscience, and omnipresence to live and walk on earth with the same limitations we have, and He did it without sinning! Jesus was not half God and half man. Jesus did not have any advantage over us because He existed with God the Father before He came to earth. He did not live from His divinity, He lived as you and I can live because He was just like we are if we are born again.

Stay with me and we will continue to unravel this very important truth. If Jesus didn't need to come as one hundred percent man, there would have been no need for Him to be born a baby, grow up, learn and mature, etc. He could have just appeared fully as God on earth, fulfill His ministry, suffer the cross and be resurrected.

In John 1:1-2 it says, "In the beginning was the Word, and the Word was with God, and the Word was God. He was in the beginning with God." This is obviously speaking of Jesus. And it is clear that Jesus was not only *with* God but also *was* God. He was divine; there is no question about it. Jesus is the second person of the Trinity. However, for the thirty-three years He spent on earth He lived and functioned as a man like you and I.

SON OF MAN

In Daniel 7, the Messiah (Jesus) is referred to as the Son of Man. Interestingly, in the four gospel accounts,

Jesus referred to Himself as the Son of Man 80 times but as the Son of God just 25 times. This would have been a term that the Jews were at least somewhat familiar with. Jesus used the term "Son of Man" more than three times as often as "Son of God." It seems probable that He wanted people to understand that He saw Himself as a man and wanted us to know that He was identifying Himself with us. The term "Son of Man" is a phrase that describes Jesus' humanity. While fully divine, He was also truly human in all respects. And having emptied Himself of the exercise of His divinity, He took on the full likeness of human weakness and limitations. It is also interesting that in Daniel 8, Daniel is also referred to as the son of man. So, in the same book of Daniel, the term "son of man" is a reference to Jesus and Daniel, not Jesus exclusively.

BROTHER OF MAN

Note the following passages that emphasize Jesus' identity as a man. "Therefore, He had to be made like His brethren in all things..." (Hebrews 2:17). To be a brother means to be related to someone—the same family DNA. We are not brothers with the fish of the sea, the birds of the air, or any other creature. Jesus was born like all those who are born again. Jesus is our Messiah, but He is also our brother. Romans 8:29 identifies Jesus as "the firstborn among many brethren." He was born into this world in a born-again condition as the first type of a new creation. At that time, He was the only begotten Son of God. After the resurrection, He became the firstborn among many brothers. His nature, his very DNA, is in us. We are blood brothers, having the same Father.

JESUS LEARNED AND GREW AS A MAN

Jesus grew in wisdom, stature and favor, with God and man.

Luke 2:52

If Jesus lived and functioned from His deity as God, He would have had no need to grow in wisdom because He would have been born with all wisdom. This scripture also says that Jesus grew in favor with God. The word for favor here is *grace*. The Bible tells us that Jesus grew in grace. Amazing! Again, if He lived as God, He would have had no need to grow in favor or grace because He would have already possessed all of it.

In the book of Isaiah, there is even a more startling truth about Jesus and His humanity. Many theologians and commentators have a very difficult time with this passage and do not relate it to Jesus. But when you read it, who else could it be speaking about? Isaiah prophesied that Jesus would have to learn to choose the difference between good and evil while He was still a child.

Therefore the Lord Himself will give you a sign: Behold, a virgin will be with child and bear a son, and she will call His name Immanuel. He will eat curds and honey at the time He knows enough to refuse evil and choose good. For before the boy will know enough to refuse evil and choose good, ...

Isaiah 7:14-16

This is a fascinating scripture because it is one of many scriptures proving that Jesus was truly human in all respects. He had to learn and grow as we do. He wasn't born knowing all truth, having all grace or wisdom. I know this may be very difficult for some to believe. Either this scripture is speaking of Jesus or there was another virgin birth of a man called Immanuel (meaning God with us).

From this scripture, we see that Jesus didn't know who He was from birth. It seems likely that Jesus had been learning His identity as the Son of God slowly over the years. As far as Scripture tells us, we know that Jesus waited 30 years before he received spoken validation of His identity from His Heavenly Father.

> *After being baptized, Jesus came up immediately from the water; and behold, the heavens were opened, and he saw the Spirit of God descending as a dove and lighting on Him, and behold, a voice out of the heavens said, "This is My beloved Son, in whom I am well-pleased."*
>
> Matthew 3:16-17

It was this declaration and affirmation that propelled Jesus forward into public ministry and gave Him the momentum to do all that He did in the next three years; face the temptation in the wilderness, live His extraordinary life, perform life-changing miracles, and teach established truth with a fresh, new revelation.

Jesus Himself needed affirmation of His identity at the beginning, in the midst of, and at the end of His ministry. It is interesting to note that the words God used, "This is my beloved son in whom I am well pleased!" are the same words a Jewish father uses during the Bar Mitzvah ceremony. The Bar Mitzvah ceremony (Bat

Mitzvah for a female) is the point in a Jewish boy's life, age 13, that he enters manhood, becomes personally responsible and attains legal rights. These words could not be spoken over a child of illegitimate or questionable birth. Jesus' step-father, Joseph, could not have been the one who spoke this. Only Jesus' true Father could speak these words over Him. These words gave a child the validation and empowerment they needed for life. This gave Jesus confidence and strength to walk in His true identity in ministry and fulfill His destiny on earth. The Jews that were present and heard these words spoken would have known exactly what was taking place.

Speaking of the baptism of Jesus, Scripture says:

> *Jesus, full of the Holy Spirit, returned from the Jordan and was led around by the Spirit in the wilderness.*
>
> Luke 4:1

> *And Jesus returned to Galilee in the power of the Spirit, and news about Him spread through all the surrounding district.*
>
> Luke 4:14

If Jesus needed the revelation of His identity and validation from His Father, we desperately need it.

Notice that Jesus was "full of the Spirit" after His baptism as he headed to His temptation in the wilderness but returned "in the power of the Spirit." If Jesus had been born "full of the Spirit," He wouldn't have needed to become full after He was baptized, nor would he have come forth in any more power than usual after His temptation.

It seems that as Jesus was growing up prior to His public ministry, He wasn't full of the Spirit, nor was He living in the full power of the Holy Spirit. Rather, it appears that He was in a growth process even as we are.

If Jesus needed the revelation of His identity and validation from His Father, we *desperately* need it.

JESUS WAS TEMPTED

In James 1:13 it says that God cannot be tempted by evil; however, we know that Jesus was tempted by evil in the wilderness. If He was living as God, He would have been unable to be tempted. It is true that the word for *tempted* also means *tested*. So, we can say that Jesus was tested in the wilderness by Satan, who used temptation to test Him. Either way, the result is the same.

Again, in Hebrews, we see that Jesus has been tempted as we are:

> *For we do not have a high priest who cannot sympathize with our weaknesses, but One who has been tempted in all things as we are, yet without sin.*
>
> Hebrews 4:15

God cannot be tempted by evil and God cannot sin. However, Jesus was tempted. This means it was possible for Him to sin, but He chose not to. If it were not possible for Jesus to sin, then this would not have been a real temptation or test, whichever way you prefer to look at it.

JESUS IS FLESH AND BLOOD

Hebrews says that:

> *Therefore, since the children share in flesh and blood, He Himself likewise also partook of the same, that through death He might render powerless him who had the power of death, that is, the devil, ...*
>
> Hebrews 2:14

The words "flesh and blood" define Jesus' humanity. He was truly flesh and blood, fully human in all respects. Also, notice in Romans 8:3, "...God...sending His own Son in the likeness of sinful flesh and as an offering for sin..." and in 2 Corinthians 5:21, "He made Him who knew no sin to be sin on our behalf, so that we might become the righteousness of God in Him."

And finally, Hebrews tells us:

> *But we do see Him who was made for a little while lower than the angels, namely, Jesus, because of the suffering of death crowned with glory and honor, so that by the grace of God He might taste death for everyone.*
>
> Hebrews 2:9

A little lower than the angels! What?! The phrase "being made for a little while lower than the angels" is describing the humility of the incarnation of Jesus. We know that God is not lower than angels, neither can God die. So, Jesus took on flesh and blood in order that He might suffer, be tempted, and even die.

Jesus' Identity Challenged

It is interesting to note that Jesus was challenged in the area of identity more than any other, which shows the importance of knowing the source and basis of our identity. One clear example is His temptation in the wilderness. Satan questioned His identity by attempting to create doubt about whether He was the Son of God.

> *And the devil said to Him, "If You are the Son of God, tell this stone to become bread."*
>
> *And he led Him to Jerusalem and had Him stand on the pinnacle of the temple, and said to Him, "If You are the Son of God, throw Yourself down from here; ..."*
>
> Luke 4:3, 9

The word *if* was intended to subtly create doubt in Jesus' mind. We may believe a thing to be true, but the word *if* introduces doubt. It asks us to suppose it is not true. The word *if* can play on our human minds and lead us to feel that we must prove something to be true or false. It can make us feel that something is wrong or incomplete. It can even make us doubt the validity of something we've always believed. Satan was indeed "more crafty" than other creatures (ref. Genesis 3:1).

The challenge Jesus faced from the devil was twofold. First, He was tempted to doubt that He had really heard from His Father about His identity. And second, He was tempted to prove His identity by His own efforts. We are also tempted to not only question whether we heard correctly from God about who He says we are but also to use our own efforts to prove ourselves to others, ourselves, even to God. Scripture says that Jesus did not entrust himself to man because He knew what was in man's heart (ref. John 2:24). Jesus knew that unregenerate man is fickle, giving allegiance and praise one day but rejection and criticism the next.

Jesus' identity as Messiah Son of God was also doubted and mocked by his own biological half-brothers (ref. John 7:3-5). We also find that many in His hometown did not believe He was the Messiah (ref. Luke 4:22). He was questioned more than once by the Pharisees about His identity. In fact, the chief priests and Pharisees contrived to have Him crucified because He refused to back down from His claims regarding His identity and purpose. The very reason Jesus was arrested and crucified was for His identity.

In the Roman Empire, when a criminal was condemned to death by crucifixion, they would write on a placard what the criminal was condemned for. This placard was carried before him or hung around his neck. The inscription was called a title (*titlos* in Greek).

> *Pilate also wrote an inscription and put it on the cross. It was written, "Jesus The Nazarene, The King Of The Jews." Therefore many of the Jews read this inscription, for the place where Jesus was crucified was near the city; and it was written in Hebrew, Latin and in Greek. So the chief priests of the Jews were saying to Pilate, "Do not write, 'The King of the Jews'; but that He said, 'I am King of the Jews.'" Pilate answered, "What I have written I have written."*
>
> John 19:19-22

Notice the chief priests said to Pilate, "Do not write, 'The King of the Jews' on the placard, but rather that, "He said, 'I am King of the Jews.'" The chief priests weren't bothered by Pilate writing; Jesus the Nazarene on the placard, which declares his humanity. But Pilate prophetically declared, "What I have written, I have written."

The truth declared by the mouth of a pagan governor and written by the hand of a Roman soldier clearly testifies of Jesus' regal identity for all eternity. The placard nailed to the cross over Jesus' head read what He was condemned to death by crucifixion for; KING OF THE JEWS. His identity. Jesus wasn't a king who became a son. He was the Son of God and therefore the King.

TESTIMONIES AFTER THE RESURRECTION

In Acts 2:22, Peter preached his first sermon in which he describes Jesus. Let's see how he did this.

> *"Men of Israel, listen to these words: Jesus the Nazarene, a man attested to you by God with miracles and wonders and signs which God performed through Him in your midst..."*
>
> Acts 2:22

First, he said "Jesus, the Nazarene." A Nazarene was a person from Nazareth. So, Peter was linking Jesus to a town on earth just like any other human being. He didn't say, "Jesus from Heaven." Next, Peter called Jesus, "a man." It is noteworthy that he didn't call Him God. Instead, Peter said Jesus was a man just like us, and lived in a town just like us. Then Peter said, "God performed," e.g., God the Father is the one who worked the miracles, wonders and signs through Jesus. In other words, he didn't say that Jesus was the one who initiated or worked the miracles from His own power or volition or even of His own deity. In reading Peter's entire sermon, he went on to say that it was God who raised Jesus from the dead; Jesus didn't raise Himself from the dead. Then at the end of the sermon, in verse 36, Peter said,

> *"Therefore, let all the house of Israel know for certain that God has made Him both Lord and Christ – this Jesus whom you crucified."*

God the Father made Jesus the man both Lord and Christ. Jesus did every one of his miracles, taught every lesson, prophesied every word God spoke to Him, and prayed every prayer as a man led by His Father and empowered by the Holy Spirit. The Father did the works through Jesus.

In Luke 3:23, we find the genealogy of Jesus. Luke walks back Jesus' lineage all the way to the first man, Adam, and then to God. Showing Jesus is a human with a human lineage, verse 38 concludes this exhaustive recitation with these words: "the son of Enosh, the son of Seth, the son of Adam, the son of God."

JESUS DID NOT INITIATE HIS OWN WORDS AND WORKS

> *For I have come down from heaven, not to do My own will, but the will of Him who sent Me.*
>
> John 6:38

> *Therefore Jesus answered and was saying to them, "Truly, truly, I say to you, the Son can do nothing of Himself, unless it is something He*

> sees the Father doing; for whatever the Father does, these things the Son also does in like manner."
>
> John 5:19

I want to reiterate that Jesus did not act out of His own will, desire, authority or power. He only did what He saw the Father doing. Jesus was completely dependent on and obedient to the Father. The words *do*, *does* and *doing* in John 5:19 are Greek words that can also mean "to create" or "to make." So, this verse could read this way:

> The Son can create nothing of Himself, unless it is something He sees the Father creating; for whatever the Father creates, these things the Son also creates in like manner.
>
> John 5:19 (paraphrased)

A similar thought is echoed in verse 30.

> "I can do nothing on My own initiative. As I hear, I judge; and My judgment is just, because I do not seek My own will, but the will of Him who sent Me."
>
> John 5:30

Jesus spoke only those things He heard the Father speak. Here are a couple more scriptures.

> So Jesus said, "... I do nothing on My own initiative, but I speak these things as the Father taught Me."
>
> John 8:28

> *"For I did not speak on My own initiative, but the Father Himself who sent Me has given Me a commandment as to what to say and what to speak."*
>
> John 12:49

Again, Jesus did not do what He wanted to do; He was completely dependent on the will of His Father, just as you and I ought to be. This is such an encouraging truth. It means we can live as Jesus did. I pray the revelation of the power that dwells within us as believers gives each of us a true vision of our identity as born-again sons and daughters of God.

JESUS DISCOVERS HIS IDENTITY

How did Jesus discover His identity? Did He just know instinctively, or did He need to discover the truth about Himself as we do? If He knew that God was His Father from birth, and He didn't need to learn who He was, then He had an advantage that we do not have.

We have scriptural proof that Jesus discovered the truth about Himself from His Father directly and from the Scriptures. One of the earliest examples is found in Isaiah 50.

> *The Lord GOD has given Me the tongue of disciples,*
> *That I may know how to sustain the weary one with a word.*
> *He awakens Me morning by morning,*
> *He awakens My ear to listen as a disciple.*
> *The Lord GOD has opened My ear;*
> *And I was not disobedient nor did I turn back.*
>
> Isaiah 50:4-5

Jesus said He received discipleship from His Father. He learned who He was and what His purpose was directly from His Father. In Luke 2:49, we see that this is true.

> *"Why is it that you were looking for Me? Did you not know that I had to be in my Father's house?"*
>
> Luke 2:49

Jesus was twelve years old at this point and took on responsibility for His actions when He was questioned by His parents. We know from this passage that by age twelve, Jesus knew who His Father was and what His purpose would be. We also know from Isaiah 50 that Jesus learned His identity from His Father at an early age. In chapter 4 of Luke, we have another clue as to how Jesus discovered His identity.

> *And He came to Nazareth, where He had been brought up; and as was His custom, He entered the synagogue on the Sabbath, and stood up to read. And the book of the prophet Isaiah was handed to Him. And He opened the book, and found the place where it was written,*
> *"The Spirit of the Lord is upon Me*
> *Because He anointed Me to preach the gospel to the poor.*
> *He has sent Me to proclaim release to the captives,*
> *And recovery of sight to the blind,*
> *To set free those who are oppressed,*
> *To proclaim the favorable year of the Lord."*
>
> Luke 4:16-19

In verse 16, it says that Jesus had a custom of going to the synagogue and reading from the scriptures. On this occasion, He stood up and read from the passage that declared His messianic identity, which He proceeded to announce was fulfilled in their hearing...on that day!

It is reasonable to assume that at some point in Jesus' boyhood His mother told Him the story of how the angel of the Lord came to her one night and gave her a promise that she would have a child without her lying with a man. And that this child would be the Messiah, who was in fact Him. However, scripture does not tell us that this is the case.

Jesus clearly was raised in a devout home where God was honored, and the synagogue was attended regularly and where He read from the scriptures. As His public ministry opened, He returned to His hometown synagogue in Nazareth and boldly revealed His identity as Israel's Messiah. While His messianic identity may have been told Him by His mother, it is clear that her witness only confirmed the revelatory witness of the Father and the Spirit to His heart, which is how our identity must be discovered as well. Jesus learned of His identity and purpose from two sources: Directly from His Father and from scripture. John the Baptist also quoted scripture, Isaiah 40:3, when answering the question of his identity.

> *This is the testimony of John, when the Jews sent to him priests and Levites from Jerusalem to ask him, "Who are you?" And he confessed and did not deny, but confessed, "I am not the Christ." They asked him, "What then? Are you Elijah?" And he*

> *said, "I am not." "Are you the Prophet?" And he answered, "No." Then they said to him, "Who are you, so that we may give an answer to those who sent us? What do you say about yourself?" He said, "I am a voice of one crying in the wilderness, 'Make straight the way of the Lord,' as Isaiah the prophet said.*
>
> John 1:19-23.

In Hebrews, we are given more understanding that Jesus discovered His identity in scripture.

> "THEN I SAID, "BEHOLD, I HAVE COME (IN THE SCROLL OF THE BOOK IT IS WRITTEN OF ME) TO DO YOUR WILL, O GOD."
>
> Hebrews 10:7

Jesus was taunted, questioned and eventually killed because of His identity. We should also be aware that as we come into a more complete revelation of our true identity as sons and daughters of God, we will be challenged just as He was. But we can be assured that as we stand on God's revealed truth about who He says we are, we too shall overcome the enemy's taunts and subtle suggestions to doubt ourselves. If the enemy challenged Jesus in the area of identity, how much more will he challenge us!

6

A NEW CREATION

Therefore if anyone is in Christ, he is a new creature; the old things passed away; behold, new things have come.

2 Corinthians 5:17

SINCE THE BEGINNING OF TIME, man has sought the answers to three important questions:

Who am I?
Why am I here?
Where am I going?

The answer to the first question, "Who am I?" reveals our identity. The answer to the second, "Why am I here?" reveals our purpose. And the answer to the third, "Where am I going?" reveals our destiny.

Significantly, if you know the correct answer to the first question, the answers to the remaining two will unfold. Conversely, if our answer to the first question is not founded in truth, then the answers to the other two questions will most likely not be true. Therefore, we need to know the correct answer to who or what are we.

The best place to begin our journey of discovering who we are is in the place of truth—the Scriptures—and the genesis of creation. If we begin at the correct place, we will arrive at the correct conclusion. If we begin at a different place, we will inevitably arrive at a different conclusion. It all begins with God our Creator.

> *If we begin at the correct place, we will arrive at the correct conclusion.*

As we know, Adam was the first created human. *Adam* means humankind. Then from Adam came the first woman, Eve. God blessed them to be fruitful and multiply. Adam is the human father of all mankind, and Eve is the mother of all mankind. God placed Adam and Eve in a garden of indescribable beauty, provision and intimacy. God told Adam that he could eat from any tree in the Garden except the Tree of the Knowledge of Good and Evil. Adam was warned by God that if he ate from it, he would surely die. In the Hebrew language, the fact that Adam would surely die is stated in the strongest terms. Death is the consequence of choosing to eat from the wrong tree, thereby sinning.

The basic definition of death is separation. Death is not only a single event, as when our heart stops, but a way of living a type of life that God wanted to protect us from experiencing. In other words, a life separated from the life Jesus said He came to give us. In John 10:10 Jesus said, "I came that they may have life (*zoe*) and have it abundantly." He didn't come to give us physical life (*bios*); we already have that. He came to give us (*zoe*) life, a quality of life, an abundance of life. *Zoe* is the same life Jesus lived; it is the life of God. Why did Jesus come to give us life? Because man was living in a state of death. Look at what it says in Ephesians 2:

> *And you were dead in your trespasses and sins, in which you formerly walked according to the course of this world, according to the prince of the power of the air, of the spirit that is now working in the sons of disobedience. Among them we too all formerly lived in the lusts of our flesh, indulging the desires of the flesh and of the mind, and were by nature children of wrath, even as the rest.*
>
> Ephesians 2:1-3

It tells us we were dead, and we were by "nature" children of wrath. Our nature was corrupted and caused us to exist in death because we lost *zoe* life when Adam sinned.

This is illustrated in the Prodigal Son story found in Luke 15:11-31. Twice the father in this story makes the statement that the son who left his father along with his inheritance was dead and then came to life again, that he was lost and then was found.

When Adam and Eve sinned by eating the forbidden fruit, the curse of death was released and introduced into all of creation (ref. Romans 5:12). As a result of disobeying God's command, Adam and Eve abdicated their authority and dominion of the earth and literally handed it over to Satan. We know that because when Satan was tempting Jesus in the wilderness, he said all the kingdoms of the world had been handed over to him (ref. Luke 4:6.) We know Adam and Eve didn't die physically at that moment of their sin, but rather became separated from the *zoe* (life of God) life that God intended them to have. Evidence of this is the consequence of their sin as laid out by God in Genesis 3.

> *To the woman He said,*
> *"I will greatly multiply*
> *Your pain in childbirth,*
> *In pain you will bring forth children;*
> *Yet your desire will be for your husband,*
> *And he will rule over you."*
> *Then to Adam He said, "Because you have listened to the voice of your wife, and have eaten from the tree about which I commanded you, saying, 'You shall not eat from it';*
> *Cursed is the ground because of you;*
> *In toil you will eat of it*
> *All the days of your life.*
> *"Both thorns and thistles it shall grow for you;*
> *And you will eat the plants of the field;*
> *By the sweat of your face*
> *You will eat bread,*
> *Till you return to the ground,*
> *Because from it you were taken;*
> *For you are dust,*
> *And to dust you shall return."*
>
> Genesis 3:16-19

As a result of the corruption of death, man's nature was corrupted and separated from an intimate union with God. Yet God was still their Creator. He still loved them, cared for them and provided for them. However, Adam and Eve's nature was now corrupted as a result of losing the *zoe* life of God.

This condition of death includes, but not limited to: aging, sickness, disease, poverty, lack, guilt, shame, fear, hopelessness, depression, confusion, chaos, eventual physical death, etc. Notice husbands ruling over wives is also part of the curse of death. Death is a perversion of the *zoe* life we are created to live and enjoy. God did not create evil. Evil is a perversion of that which God created as good and holy. It is a consequence of disobedience. The condition of our world with all sorts of evil: murder, rape, thefts, hate, etc., is a result of man's rejection of God. God gave man authority over the earth, and the condition of it is because of man, not God. God did not create man to die or to experience a life of death. Scripture tells us that death is the last enemy to be destroyed (ref. 1 Cor. 15:26), so until then, we all live with the constant reminder of the consequence of this curse of death; aging and eventual physical death, plus all the evil that exists in the world.

Adam and Eve were removed from the Garden of Eden and not allowed back in. Eden was not only a real place but is also a picture of all that God intended for man, animals, and all of nature. The word *garden* means "enclosure." The word *Eden* means "pleasure and delight." The Garden of Eden is an enclosure of pleasure and delight. In part, it represents the *zoe* type of life, union with God and the Sabbath rest. When God placed Adam in the Garden, it literally means: "He set man at rest in the Garden." Even today, people use the term Eden to describe a heavenly paradise. The Garden was a type and shadow of the Kingdom of Heaven on earth—a taste of what it will be like after Jesus returns, and His Kingdom is fully manifested. God gave man the authority to expand this Garden, His Kingdom, on the earth.

We all yearn for the ideal place of peace and beauty that Eden represents. God intended that He and man experience intimate communion, bountiful provision and an eternal cohabitation. But now, because of the curse that sin released and the terrible consequence that death has on humanity, such intimacy was impossible. So, God established a temporary fix until Jesus came to take care of the sin problem forever. He covered Adam and Eve with the skin of animals.

Because of Adam's sin, all of his offspring are incapable of experiencing the life of God, having intimate, spirit to Spirit communion with God or receiving the inheritance God planned. This is one reason why God hates sin so much. It not only violates His holy nature (and ours), but it also has progressively negative effects on man, and ultimately, it keeps man eternally separated from God. Aging and death are lifelong devastating examples of the effects that sin has on us. Our hearts yearn for a restoration of what was lost. We have been cut off from the very one who is our life source.

It should be obvious that God did not create Adam with a corrupted nature. But after he sinned, his nature became corrupted and thereafter, his corrupted seed or DNA transmitted that nature to all his descendants. So, all who are born after him, which is everyone, inherited that corrupted nature. Until a person chooses to become born again by receiving Christ Jesus, they continue to have a corrupted nature they inherited from Adam. This corrupted nature keeps us separated from God, and the provision and relationship He originally planned for us (as illustrated in the Prodigal Son story). That is why Romans 5:12 says, "Therefore, just as through one man sin entered into the world, and death through sin, ...so death spread to all men, because all sinned."

When any man is "in" Adam and not "in" Christ, he is still dominated by the corrupted nature. He is an "old creature" under the control of Satan's domain (ref. 2 Cor. 5:17, Col. 1:13). Consider the language that John uses:

> *By this the <u>children of God</u> and the <u>children of the devil</u> are obvious: anyone who does not practice righteousness is not of God, nor the one who does not love his brother.*
>
> 1 John 3:10 (emphasis added)

There is no middle ground with God. We are either a child of the devil or a child of God. This may be a difficult concept to swallow, and it certainly isn't politically correct since it is a universal belief that every human is a child of God. However, Scripture does not confirm this belief. Scripture makes a clear distinction between the children of God and the children of the devil. To us, it may seem like strong language, but the Bible calls those who are not born again "children of the devil." It clearly states that the division between the children of God and the children of the devil is "obvious." Here are two other scripture references;

> *"You are of your father the devil, and you want to do the desires of your father. He was a murderer from the beginning, and does not stand in the truth, because there is no truth in him. Whenever he speaks a lie, he speaks from his own nature; for he is a liar, and the father of lies."*
>
> John 8:44

> *Do you not know that when you present yourselves to someone as slaves for obedience, you are slaves of the one whom you obey, either of sin resulting in death, or of obedience resulting in righteousness?*
>
> Romans 6:16

Every human being is a creation of God, but not all are His children.

> *But as many as received Him, to them He gave the right to become children of God, even to those who believe in His name...*
>
> John 1:12

Even logically, we know that we cannot become something that we already are, so we realize we must "become" a child of God since we aren't born one. When we repent or turn to Jesus and receive Him as our Lord and Savior, committing our lives to Him, God removes our old nature, replaces it with a new holy nature created in His image according to His likeness, and we become a child of God. Just like when God breathed into Adam and he became a living being, God breathes His Spirit (His life and nature) into us at the new birth.

WHAT ABOUT JESUS?

Through each successive generation, sin traveled through the seed of Adam, to our human fathers to us (ref. Romans 5:12). It is the seed of our biological father that transfers this corrupted nature. This is the reason Jesus did not have a human father. God was His Father so that a corrupt nature would not be passed down to Jesus. God's nature was in Jesus. God the Father was the one who determined Jesus' identity, not a human man. Jesus was not born in sin. He was sinless, although all of our sin was placed upon Him and then nailed to the cross.

Jesus was actually born in the same condition we are when we are born again. He did not have a corrupt nature. He was like Adam when Adam was first created. That also means that Jesus, just like Adam, could have chosen to sin but He never did. The word *Adam* means "humankind or mankind." The Bible calls Jesus the last Adam (humankind) in 1 Corinthians 15:45. God intended for His (God's) nature to travel through Adam to all men. However, when Adam sinned, causing his nature to become corrupt, instead of God's pure, holy nature passing on to mankind, a corrupt nature passed on to all men. This is why Adam and Eve were removed from the Garden of Eden and not allowed back in to feed on the Tree of Life and live forever in that corrupted nature (ref. Genesis 3:22). Jesus, who is the Tree of Life, came as the last Adam so that once again, God's nature can pass to all men who receive Jesus as Lord and Savior of their life by becoming born again.

> *Therefore, just as through one man sin entered into the world, and death through sin, and so death spread to all men, because all sinned for until the Law sin was in the world; but sin is not imputed when there is no law. Nevertheless death reigned from Adam until Moses, even over those who had not sinned in the likeness of the offense of Adam, who is a type of Him who was to come. But the free gift is not like the transgression. For if by the transgression of the one the many died, much more did the grace of*

God and the gift by the grace of the one Man, Jesus Christ, abound to the many. And the gift is not like that which came through the one who sinned; for on the one hand the judgment arose from one transgression resulting in condemnation, but on the other hand the free gift arose from many transgressions resulting in justification. For if by the transgression of the one, death reigned through the one, much more those who receive the abundance of grace and of the gift of righteousness will reign in life through the One, Jesus Christ. So then as through one transgression there resulted condemnation to all men, even so through one act of righteousness there resulted justification of life to all men. For as through the one man's disobedience the many were made sinners, even so through the obedience of the One the many will be made righteous.

Romans 5:12-19

Two Births

Speaking with Nicodemus, Jesus said, "Truly, truly, I say to you, unless one is born again, he cannot see the kingdom of God." Jesus instructed this teacher of Israel concerning two separate births. John 3:6 says, "That which is born of the flesh is flesh, and that which is born of the Spirit is spirit." The first birth is the natural, biological birth. The second is a spiritual rebirth whereby a person is recreated in the image of God, according to His likeness. He is actually born into His family. All people are born into sin, separated from God and eternally lost until they receive Jesus Christ and are born again or born from above. This is the purpose of the new birth: to take a sinful, "old creature" who is alienated from God and transform them into a righteous, "new creature" who is re-created in the image and likeness of God's Son.

This new birth is further illustrated when a Roman soldier discovered that Jesus (the last Adam) had already died on the cross, and he stuck his sword in Jesus' side. Water and blood flowed from Jesus.

> *But one of the soldiers pierced His side with a spear, and immediately blood and water came out.*
>
> John 19:34

This refers us back to when God put Adam to sleep and took a rib or a side of him and created Eve. At the time of Jesus' death, when blood and water flowed from His side, He was giving birth to His Bride; sons of God.

> *Jesus answered, "Truly, truly, I say to you, unless one is born of water and the Spirit he cannot enter into the kingdom of God. "That which is born of the flesh is flesh, and that which is born of the Spirit is spirit. "Do not be amazed that I said to you, 'You must be born again.' "The wind blows where it wishes and you hear the sound of it, but do not know where it comes from and where it is going; so is everyone who is born of the Spirit."*
>
> John 3:5-8

> *This is the One who came by water and blood, Jesus Christ; not with the water only, but with the water and*

> with the blood. It is the Spirit who testifies, because the Spirit is the truth. For there are three that testify: the Spirit and the water and the blood; and the three are in agreement.
>
> 1 John 5:6-8

As we have already stated, not everyone is a child of God. We must be born again. Let's look closely at what happens to us when we are born again. Corinthians states:

> Therefore if any man is in Christ, he is a new creature; the old things have passed away; behold, new things have come.
>
> 2 Corinthians 5:17

We enter a new family relationship — the family of God — and God becomes our Father.

We learn from this verse that one who is "in Christ" is a new creature or a new creation. The word *creature* means "a product of God's handiwork." When we are born again, we become a completely different creation. We are not the same as we once were. Our nature (identity) changes because we receive a new spirit. We receive the nature of God which is the "new things" the verse mentions, and our old corrupt nature, "old things," is removed. We literally become part of another race of people. There are only two races of humans — God's children and those who are not. When we become God's child, we receive His nature just like when we were born physically, we received the nature of our parents. We enter a new family relationship — the family of God — and God becomes our Father.

Some believe that when we are born again, we still have an old sin nature, the old man or flesh, as well as the new re-created spirit (the new man). In other words, we now have a dual nature. However, there is no precedent in God's created order for this. He has not created a bird, fish or another animal with a dual nature, much less a human being. To have a dual nature, one good and the other evil, violates the intent and the law of God. The Apostle Paul warns believers:

> *Do not be bound together with unbelievers; for what partnership have righteousness and lawlessness, or what fellowship has light with darkness?*
>
> 2 Corinthians 6:14

There are many other references in scripture, both the Old and New Covenants convey this same truth. Even in nature it is not light and dark at the same time. An apple tree is not also an orange tree. Neither is a bird also a snake. Two natures cannot coexist in the same body simultaneously. The inconsistent way the popular NIV Bible translation interprets the word *flesh* has contributed to this misunderstanding.

To have a dual nature with two opposing natures warring within us would not be good news. That would leave us in a vulnerable condition that can lead to having more problems than we had before we were born again. It sounds more like something the devil would try to do than God. As a matter of fact, this is what a demon-possessed person is like.

WHAT DID THE APOSTLE PAUL ACTUALLY SAY?

For we know that the Law is spiritual; but I am of flesh, sold into bondage to sin. For that which I am doing, I do not understand; for I am not practicing what I would like to do, but I am doing the very thing I hate. But if I do the very thing I do not wish to do, I agree with the Law, confessing that it is good. So now, no longer am I the one doing it, but sin which indwells me. For I know that nothing good dwells in me, that is, in my flesh; for the wishing is present in me, but the doing of the good is not. For the good that I wish, I do not do; but I practice the very evil that I do not wish. But if I am doing the very thing I do not wish, I am no longer the one doing it, but sin which dwells in me. I find then the principle that evil is present in me, the one who wishes to do good. For I joyfully concur with the law of God in the inner man, but I see a different law in the members of my body, waging war against the law of my mind, and making me a prisoner of the law of sin which is in my members. Wretched man that I am! Who will set me free from the body of this death? Thanks be to God through Jesus Christ our Lord! So then, on the one hand I myself with my mind am serving the law of God, but on the other, with my flesh the law of sin.

Romans 7:14-25

I used to read this passage of scripture for comfort because I could identify with it. It is one that many Christians reference to prove that we still have a sin nature after being born again. Yet is that really what the Apostle Paul is saying here? On the surface, it sounds like he has two natures that operate by two separate laws within him and are in a constant state of war.

Before he was born again, Paul was a Pharisee. He observed the Law with strict adherence as he says in Philippians:

> ...although I myself might have confidence even in the flesh. If anyone else has a mind to put confidence in the flesh, I far more: circumcised the eighth day, of the nation of Israel, of the tribe of Benjamin, a Hebrew of Hebrews; as to the Law, a Pharisee; as to zeal, a persecutor of the church; as to the righteousness which is in the Law, found blameless.
>
> Philippians 3:4-6

Notice how many times the word *I* is used—24 times! You see, Paul is writing this from the perspective of one who is not born again but living by the works of the Law—a religious, legalistic person, one who is not operating out of a relationship of love. In other words, he is trying to be obedient and pleasing to God in his own strength and power without Christ. This leads to being focused on the flesh (the natural), not the spiritual.

In verse 14 he says that "but I am of flesh, sold into bondage to sin." When we are born again, we are not sold into bondage to sin. That is the very thing God delivers us from! Then he says that he is doing the very thing he hates and finds that he is no longer the one doing it, but sin that indwells him. When we are born again, we are not given a "master of sin" to obey its every lust. Verse 18 says, "for I know that nothing good dwells in me." Well, if we are born again there is something great and very good in us! "Christ in you the hope of glory" (Colossian 1:27). In verse 24 he says, "Wretched man that I am." Once again, a wretched state is not the condition that we are born again into. In the same verse he says, "who will set me free from the body of this death?" He is asking who will set him free from this condition he just described. He is not saying this is what happens to us when we are born again. This would not be good news at all. This is not even in line with the character or nature of God.

We learn the answer to this wretched condition in verse twenty-five, "Thanks be to God through Jesus Christ our Lord!" Praise the Lord that it is Jesus Christ who delivers us from this wretched condition! Thank God. Because of the life, death and resurrection of Jesus Christ, we can experience the very same quality of life *(zoe)* that Jesus experienced and that He said He came to give to us.

> *The thief comes only to steal and kill and destroy;*
> *I came that they may have life* (zoe), *and have it abundantly.*
>   John 10:10 (parenthesis added)

If we believe what Paul describes in chapter 7 of Romans, that we have a dual nature and these two natures are at war with each other within us, then what was written before this in chapter 6, or what comes afterward in chapter 8, doesn't make any sense and is actually a contradiction. The problem we are faced with is not a dual nature but an unrenewed soul; mind will and emotions.

CIRCUMCISION

Prior to Jesus, entering into covenant with God was symbolized by the act of circumcision, which is a removal of the flesh from the most intimate part of the male body. Circumcision means a "cutting around" and symbolized that Israel was in covenant and intimate relationship with their God. The flesh that was cut around was in fact removed from the body. It was not just left in place to become irritated and scarred. And so, like circumcision, when we are born again, the old corrupt nature is completely removed, cut off, and a new spirit birthed within us. And that new spirit is perfect and has the nature of God Himself. Two other scriptures highlight this truth:

> *For he is not a Jew who is one outwardly, nor is circumcision that which is outward in the flesh. But he is a Jew who is one inwardly; and circumcision is that which is of the heart, by the Spirit, not by the letter; and his praise is not from men, but from God.*
>
> Romans 2:28-29

In this next scripture, it actually tells us that this new circumcision is the removal of the flesh.

> *... and in Him you were also circumcised with a circumcision made without hands, in the removal of the body of the flesh by the circumcision of Christ; having been buried with Him in baptism, in which you were also raised*

> *up with Him through faith in the working of God, who raised Him from the dead. When you were dead in your transgressions and the uncircumcision of your flesh, He made you alive together with Him, having forgiven us all our transgressions, ...*
>
> Colossians 2:11-13

It is also important to note that circumcision was performed on the male reproductive organ. It is from the male sperm that the gender of the child is determined and the corrupt nature originating from the first Adam is conveyed. Circumcision under the Old (first) Covenant was a sign of the covenant but also of reproducing a nation that belongs to God. Now, the New Covenant is established in the blood of Christ and we receive a new nature, a circumcision of the heart. This new nature is to be transferred to others as we are fruitful and multiplying, filling the earth and subduing it through making disciples of all nations (ref. Genesis 1:28, Matthew 28:18-20).

GOD'S SEED ABIDES IN US

Along with God's Spirit living within us, we all have the potential to develop Christ like character. The Apostle John talks about the new nature in a different way. He says that God's seed lives in the children of God. In Greek, the word for seed is *sperma*, from which our English word *sperm* is derived. God's seed, His sperm, contains His DNA and becomes the building blocks for the sum total of His nature to dwell in His children. This is truly amazing!

A New Creation

> *No one who is born of God practices sin, because His seed abides in him; and he cannot sin, because he is born of God.*
>
> 1 John 3:9

So, we see in examples given both by the Apostle Paul and the Apostle John that a dual nature cannot coexist in a born-again person. The terminology of circumcision is clear—the old flesh nature is cut off and a new nature from God that is holy, righteous and pure is birthed within us. It is the very same nature that Jesus has.

> *For in Him all the fullness of Deity dwells in bodily form, and in Him you have been made complete, and He is the head over all rule and authority; ...*
>
> Colossians 2:9-10

The phrase, "made complete," is one Greek word, *pleroo*, a verb which means "to make full." As children of God, we have all the potential within us in seed form to be made full, complete and mature in Christ Jesus.

A FAMILY DYNASTY

Many view the Ten Commandments (ref. Exodus 20) as merely a list of rules. Don't do this and don't touch that. And yet, at least part of the reason God gave us The Ten Commandments is to begin to reveal His nature and our true nature. When He said, "Do not murder," He revealed to us that He is not a murderer, and neither were we

---
Along with God's Spirit living within us, we all have the potential to develop Christ like character.
---

created to be murders. When He said to not have any other gods before Him and to not commit adultery, He revealed that He is faithful and that we are created to be faithful as well. He said to not steal, telling us He is not a thief and that we shouldn't be as well. Do not bear false witness—He is not a liar and we are not to be either, and so forth. Not only is He revealing who He is, but He is also telling us who He created us to be.

Jesus is our older brother as well as our Lord and Savior. When we are born again, we are now a part of the bloodline of Jesus and we know that He is called the Son of God. Hebrews 1:3 declares that "He, [Christ], is the radiance of His [God's] glory and the exact representation of His [God's] nature." Also, in John 14:8-9 when Philip asked Jesus to show them the Father, Jesus answered, "Have I been so long with you, and yet you have not come to know Me, Philip? He who has seen Me has seen the Father; how do you say, 'Show us the Father'?" So, the obvious conclusion is that since Jesus is the "exact representation" of His Father, and we have been given the same nature that Jesus has, we too are the exact representation of God's nature. That doesn't mean we always act like it or that our words and behavior reflect it perfectly, but we have the potential for it.

We belong to a royal family – the family dynasty of God.

When the Jews questioned Jesus about who He was, He answered: "I and the Father are One," (John 10:30). This angered the Jews, who picked up stones to stone Him because He made Himself out to be God. Jesus responded with a quote from Psalms 82:6.

> *Jesus answered them, "Has it not been written in your Law, 'I SAID, YOU ARE GODS'? "If he called them gods, to whom the word of God came (and the Scripture cannot be broken), do you say of Him, whom the Father sanctified and sent into the world, 'You are blaspheming,' because I said, 'I am the Son of God'?"*
>
> John 10:34-36

Fascinating! We belong to a royal family — the family dynasty of God.

Before we were born again, we lived under the "domain of darkness" (Colossians 1:13), which is ruled by Satan. The domain of darkness operates by the law of "sin and death" (Romans 8:2). However, after we are born again, God transfers us to the Kingdom of His beloved Son. His Kingdom operates by the law of the "Spirit of life (*zoe*) in Christ Jesus" (Romans 8:2 emphasis added). Ephesians elaborates further on this theme of the transfer from one kingdom to another.

> *And you were dead in your trespasses and sins, in which you formerly walked according to the course of this world, according to the prince of the power of the air, of the spirit that is now working in the sons of disobedience. Among them we too all formerly lived in the lusts of our flesh, indulging the desires of the flesh and of the mind, and were by nature children of wrath, even as the rest. But God, being rich in mercy, because of His great love with which He loved us, even when we were dead in our transgressions, made us alive together with*

> Christ (by grace you have been saved), and raised us up with Him, and seated us with Him in the heavenly places, in Christ Jesus, in order that in the ages to come He might show the surpassing riches of His grace in kindness toward us in Christ Jesus.
>
> Ephesians 2:1-7

In the new birth we receive a new nature that is created in the image of God according to His likeness. We are not the same person we once were. At the same time, we are delivered from the domain of darkness that operates under the law of sin and death and are transferred to the Kingdom of His beloved Son which operates by the law of the Spirit of life in Christ Jesus and motivated by love.

We can see that there is not only a definite change in our nature but there is also a change in relationships. God truly becomes our Father because His seed is now in us. God the Father has birthed us anew, and everything that is in Him is now in us. There is no sin nature or evil in God, nor is there any curse. The only curse that operates in the world was caused by man's sin. When we are born again, we receive the nature of God — His very DNA, and there is no curse in His bloodline! We can be free of all generational curses that may have functioned in our family line. This aspect of understanding our new identity is critical to walking in all that God has for us as well as living free from the curse that operates in the world.

> 'You shall not worship them or serve them; for I, the LORD your God, am a jealous God, visiting the iniquity of the fathers on the children, and on

> *the third and the fourth generations of those who hate Me, but showing lovingkindness to thousands, to those who love Me and keep My commandments.*
>
> Deuteronomy 5:9-10

We are not natural beings having a spiritual experience. We are spiritual beings having a natural experience.

> *I call heaven and earth to witness against you today, that I have set before you life and death, the blessing and the curse. So choose life in order that you may live, you and your descendants.*
>
> Deuteronomy 30:19

Jesus spoke about this change in relationships in the Gospel according to Matthew.

> *While He was still speaking to the multitudes, behold, His mother and brothers were standing outside seeking to speak to Him. And someone said to Him, "Behold, Your mother and Your brothers are standing outside seeking to speak to You." But He answered the one who was telling Him and said, "Who is My mother and who are My brothers?" And stretching out His hand toward His disciples, He said, "Behold, My mother and My brothers! "For whoever does the will of My Father who is in heaven, he is My brother and sister and mother."*
>
> Matthew 12:46-50

We are not to forsake our biological families. However, we must come to understand that we have a new family with a new Father and new brothers and sisters. This should change the way we relate to one another and care for each other. This is the family we will live with for all eternity.

After being born again and understanding what Jesus accomplished for us, identity is the most important truth we need to understand and receive revelation on. One reason is that our purpose is to reveal the nature of Christ Jesus that is in us to the world. This means not just telling people about Jesus but showing them Jesus. We will not be able to discover the truth about ourselves apart from scripture and the revelation from the Holy Spirit.

We are not natural beings having a spiritual experience.
We are spiritual beings having a natural experience.

7

ADOPTION

Adopt, [ə'däpt] – to legally receive another's child and make them one of your own.

THERE ARE SEVERAL SCRIPTURES that refer to us being adopted by God. We have already discussed that when a person is born again, God literally births him anew spiritually. The term "born again" means "born from above." However, these scriptures add a new concept and say that God adopts us when we are born again. So, which is it? Are we adopted by God or born of Him?

Actually, both are correct.

> *For you have not received a spirit of slavery leading to fear again, but you have received a spirit of adoption as sons by which we cry out, "Abba! Father!"*
>
> Romans 8:15

> *And not only this, but also we ourselves, having the first fruits of the Spirit, even we ourselves groan within ourselves, waiting eagerly for our adoption as sons, the redemption of our body.*
>
> Romans 8:23

> *...who are Israelites, to whom belongs the adoption as sons, and the glory and the covenants and the giving of the Law and the temple service and the promises...*
>
> Romans 9:4

> *He predestined us to adoption as sons through Jesus Christ to Himself, according to the kind intention of His will, ...*
>
> Ephesians 1:5

Adoption has different nuances in different cultures. In the United States of America, adoption means to legally receive a child into your family and make them one of your own—to give a child the position of a son or daughter with the same privileges and inheritance rights as a biological child. The birth certificate is also amended to reflect the new parents and the child's name. Even though the child is not born into the family naturally, he or she is one legally, just as if they were born biologically. Let's take a much closer look at what it means to be adopted by God.

> *But when the fullness of the time came, God sent forth His Son, born of a woman, born under the Law, in order that He might redeem those who were under the Law, that we might receive the adoption as sons.*
>
> Galatians 4:4-5

Three main cultures dominate in scripture: Hebrew, Greek and Roman. Each of these cultures had a process or ceremony that recognized the time in a boy's life when he entered manhood. During this ceremony, a son would become a legal adult with all of the status, privileges and inheritance rights of the family.

In Hebrew culture, when the son turned 13, he became a "son of the law," a legal adult and a voting member of the synagogue. In Greek culture, the male child became a legal adult at age 18. However, in Roman culture, the time wasn't so precise. The Roman father would determine the time his son would become a legal adult. This helps explain the following verse:

> *Now I say, as long as the heir is a child, he does not differ at all from a slave although he is owner of everything, but he is under guardians and managers until the date set by the father.*
> Galatians 4:1-2

At the time the Apostle Paul wrote the Book of Galatians, Galatia was part of the Roman Empire and had adopted the Roman culture. So, Paul was using an example from their culture to convey an important spiritual truth. The end of the verse says; "until the date set by the father." The date a Roman son became a legal adult was referred to as his "adoption." And that date was set by the Roman father, not according to the boy's specific age. The father would base his determination to adopt his own son however he liked. The boy may have had to prove that he was worthy of adoption. The father could have observed how his son behaved, handled money and responsibility, etc. before he would adopt him. Then the Roman father, if he chose to, would actually adopt his own biological son. Not until the Roman father adopted his son did the son receive full adult status, privileges and inheritance rights according to the law.

This custom opens our eyes to see the Apostle Paul's statement from a new and deeper perspective. God didn't just birth us. He also adopted us. How precious and valued we are to Him.

Paul continues the theme of adoption in the book of Ephesians, where he says that God "predestined us" to be adopted as sons. The word *predestined* doesn't mean that God predetermines who will be born again and who will not. It means that God predetermined or preplanned His purpose—that He would adopt everyone, male and female, who chose to be born again (just as the Roman father did) into His family with full status, privileges and inheritance rights as a child. What an incredible blessing the Father gives us! God determines beforehand that He will adopt us as his children at the moment of our new birth. He adopts both boys and girls and He doesn't wait to see how we behave, handle money and responsibility; He gives us all the inheritance rights immediately.

God didn't just birth us. He also adopted us.

Notice both verses say, "adoption as sons," not just adoption. God the Father doesn't just adopt us, He adopts us as His sons. We receive sonship, this implies receiving an inheritance as well. An important part of our inheritance is the right and authority to rule and reign as a king.

When a king of a country dies, his throne is transferred to his son, usually his eldest son. The royal

Adoption

throne stays within the family bloodline. For example, God made a covenant with David called the Davidic Covenant (ref. 2 Samuel 7:8-17). In that covenant, God said that David's throne, his rule or his kingship, would endure forever. God also said that David would be His son and He (God) would be his Father. Jesus came from the line of David, and we know He will rule and reign forever. As sons of God and joint heirs with Jesus Christ, we inherit the same things that Jesus does. That inheritance includes many blessings, promises and benefits, as well as functions and responsibilities. We are given the right to rule and reign with Christ over the earth as part of that inheritance. Jesus rules and reigns both in this world and the world to come. We are also to rule and reign in this age and the age to come. So, we see that God's original plan of having mankind (Adam) ruling over a dominion (Eden) has now been restored to all believers through Jesus. All of God's sons are empowered through Jesus' life, death and resurrection to rule and reign not only in the world to come but in this life also.

THE SPIRITUAL REALM

When we receive the adoption as sons, there is a legal transaction in the spirit realm that is not only recognized by God but also by every entity therein: the rulers, powers, world forces of darkness and wickedness (ref. Ephesians 6:12). This includes demons.

In Acts chapter 19, we find the interesting story of the Jewish chief priest's (Sceva) seven sons. These men were trying to cast out demons by merely using the name of Jesus without being born again. They had apparently seen the Apostle Paul exorcising demons using the name of Jesus and were fascinated by the power of God. However, when these seven men commanded a demon to depart from a man, the demon not only refused but answered them back. The demon's response was very telling. In it, we learn some important facts about the identity and authority of believers and also about the laws which demons recognize and must obey.

> *But also some of the Jewish exorcists, who went from place to place, attempted to name over those who had the evil spirits the name of the Lord Jesus, saying, "I adjure you by Jesus whom Paul preaches." Seven sons of one Sceva, a Jewish chief priest, were doing this. And the evil spirit answered and said to them, "I recognize, (I know), Jesus, and I know about, (I am acquainted with) Paul, but who are you?" And the man, in whom was the evil spirit, leaped on them and subdued all of them and overpowered them, so that they fled out of that house naked and wounded.*
>
> Acts 19:13-16 (parenthesis added)

Notice that the demon challenged their identity, asking "who are you?" We have no record that the seven sons answered that question, but we do understand that the end was not what the men expected as they fled naked and wounded. We learn from this that demons recognize the identity of a born-again person (child of God) and the authority that comes with it. They also know who imposters are. The implication is that the demon could have said, "I have to obey Jesus and I have to obey Paul, but, I do not have to obey you." Every demon, and Satan himself, must stay within the boundaries (law) that God has established. The way they get around this is by deceiving us into relinquishing our authority as they did with Adam and Eve in the Garden. As God said in Hosea 4:6: "My people are destroyed for a lack of knowledge." Even though the seven sons used the name of Jesus, the demons still did not have to obey. Just using the so-called correct words, even the name of Jesus, is not enough. Using repetitious words or even true words like the name of Jesus, without first being a son of God (an identity change) and exercising true faith, amounts to witchcraft. It didn't turn out well for these seven brothers.

ABBA, DADDY

> *Because you are sons, God has sent forth the Spirit of His Son into our hearts, crying, "Abba! Father!" Therefore you are no longer a slave, but a son; and if a son, then an heir through God.*
>
> Galatians 4:6-7

> We can still run to Him with open arms calling "Abba, Daddy!"

The word *Abba* is an Aramaic word meaning daddy. It is the same word Jesus used when He prayed to His father in the Garden of Gethsemane the night before His crucifixion. It is an intimate word of affection and trust.

This term shows us the heart of God. He is not satisfied with obtaining slaves or even in adopting sons who stand at a distance. He longs for sons and daughters in whom He can be intimate and shower with love, affection and an inheritance. Like little children who may not be able to pronounce all the words correctly, we can still run to Him with open arms calling "Abba, Daddy!" Father God desires family and a family dynasty that rules and reigns in this age and the one to come!

OUR INHERITANCE

And so, what is our inheritance? What did we obtain when God birthed us anew and adopted us as His sons and daughters? Most importantly, our inheritance is Him—the One and True God, the Creator of the universe! We inherit God our Father, Jesus our elder brother, King and Savior and the Holy Spirit as our personal counselor, teacher, and comforter along with all the resources of the Kingdom of Heaven. We inherit the Kingdom of God and the right to rule and reign over the earth. As the Apostle John said, Jesus came to give us an abundant life with multiplied blessings. Peter declares it in a little different way:

> ... *seeing that His divine power has granted to us <u>everything</u> pertaining to life and godliness, through the true knowledge of Him who called us by His own glory and excellence."*
> 2 Peter 1:3 (emphasis added)

By the way, that word *everything* in Greek means everything! God has granted everything to us and it comes through knowing Jesus Christ. We have access to everything the Kingdom of Heaven has to offer. It comes through our relationship with Christ Jesus. It is relational in nature, not transactional like a business dealing. We have a legal right to be called sons of God (ref. John 1:12). We receive abundant life, a new name, a new identity, relationship with the Lord, access to all Kingdom resources, and we are delegated His authority to subdue the earth and rule over it!

We also inherit the earth and the world! The earth is the land, the world is the cosmos—every created thing! *Cosmos* is the same word used in John:

> *For God so loved the world* (cosmos), *that He gave His only begotten Son, that whoever believes in Him shall not perish, but have eternal life.*
>
> John 3:16 (parenthesis added)

> *Blessed are the gentle, for they shall inherit the earth.*
>
> Matthew 5:5

> *For the promise to Abraham or to his descendants that he would be heir of the world was not through the Law, but through the righteousness of faith.*
>
> Romans 4:13

The Garden of Eden, the Promised Land, the Holy of Holies, Noah's ark, the Sabbath rest and abiding in the vine are just a few typological examples of our inheritance. Each was a place where God planned for mankind to dwell with Him in intimate communion and oneness, where we are protected and provided for, a *shalom*. *Shalom* means complete rest, harmony, wholeness, completeness and prosperity. This includes healing, physical, emotional, and spiritual.

When we are born again, we are birthed anew by God and His seed abides in us. God becomes our true Father and Abba, Daddy. We are now a part of His royal bloodline and all of the ability to have oneness with the Father and to be Christ-like in character is within us. We also receive Christ's inheritance—the blessing of the firstborn. We do not receive hand-me-downs or second best. We are co-heirs with Jesus. We actually receive the same inheritance as Jesus does!

> *… and if children, heirs also, heirs of God and fellow heirs with Christ, if indeed we suffer with Him so that we may also be glorified with Him.*
> Romans 8:17

After the resurrection, Jesus is no longer the only begotten Son of God. He became the firstborn among many brethren, as we are told in Romans.

> *For those whom He foreknew, He also predestined to become conformed to the image of His Son, so that He would be the firstborn among many brethren; …*
> Romans 8:29

BIRTHRIGHT AND BLESSING OF THE FIRSTBORN

There is much to be said about birthright and blessing of the firstborn. There is also plenty of scripture on the topic. I will just mention a few stories from scripture about brothers and their birthright. We have already

Adoption

discussed the two sons in the Prodigal Son story, although I will refer to them again here.

Let's look at another set of brothers, Jacob and Esau. Their story begins in Genesis 25. Jacob and Esau are twin brothers and sons of Isaac and Rebekah. Isaac is the promised son of Abraham and Sarah. Esau was the firstborn by just seconds as Jacob came out holding onto Esau's heel. We will pick up the story in verse 27:

> *When the boys grew up, Esau became a skillful hunter, a man of the field, but Jacob was a peaceful man, living in tents. Now Isaac loved Esau, because he had a taste for game, but Rebekah loved Jacob. When Jacob had cooked stew, Esau came in from the field and he was famished; and Esau said to Jacob, "Please let me have a swallow of that red stuff there, for I am famished." Therefore, his name was called Edom. But Jacob said, "First sell me your birthright." Esau said, "Behold, I am about to die; so of what use then is the birthright to me?" And Jacob said, "First swear to me"; so he swore to him, and sold his birthright to Jacob. Then Jacob gave Esau bread and lentil stew; and he ate and drank and rose and went on his way. Thus, Esau despised his birthright.*
>
> Genesis 25:27-34

Esau came in from hunting and found Jacob had made some stew. Having hunted all day, Esau was very hungry. Apparently, he didn't kill any game that day. Esau asked Jacob for some stew, but Jacob wanted to make a deal instead. He wanted Esau's birthright before he shared his stew. Esau was the firstborn son; therefore, he had a legal right to the birthright.

The birthright in Hebrew culture was a position of high honor within the family. The firstborn male child obtained the birthright simply by being born first. God stated this in Deuteronomy 1:17: "But he shall acknowledge the firstborn, the son of the unloved, by giving him a double portion of all that he has, for he is the beginning of his strength; to him belongs the right of the firstborn."

> *Jesus exercised the authority of His birthright while crucified on the cross moments before He was to die.*

In Numbers 3:13, the Lord said the firstborn belonged to Him. The birthright included receiving a double portion of inheritance along with authority over the rest of the family. He was the priest of the family and would also inherit the judicial authority of the father. We see a glimpse of this when Jesus, as the firstborn son, made provision for His mother, Mary, while in excruciating pain dying on the cross. Think of that: Jesus exercised the authority of His birthright while crucified on the cross moments before He was to die. That is how important and serious the position of the firstborn is.

In a royal family, the firstborn male son would typically assume the throne as king when the father died. As we see in 2 Chronicles:

> *Their father gave them many gifts of silver, gold and precious things, with fortified cities in*

> *Judah, but he gave the kingdom to Jehoram because he was the firstborn.*
>
> 2 Chronicles 21:3

In just this brief summary, we can see that being the firstborn came with a lot of rights and privileges in the family. It was a high honor of great value and Jacob knew this, but Esau apparently didn't think so. Jacob wanted his brother's birthright and he devised a plan to get it. It was a birthright for food deal. Esau had the birthright and Jacob had the food. So, Jacob asked Esau for the birthright in exchange for some stew. Esau replied; "Behold, I am about to die; so of what use then is the birthright to me?" Wow! His reply made it obvious that he did not value his birthright. Esau traded his birthright for a single meal! In a similar way, Adam and Eve handed over their birthright for food, a piece of fruit. It seems that food is always getting us humans in trouble.

In Genesis 25:34 it says: "Thus, Esau despised his birthright." For the temporary gratification of his flesh, Esau viewed his birthright as worthless. Temporary gratification of the flesh, the bait of sin that leads to death. The writer of the book of Hebrews calls Esau immoral and godless.

> *... that there be no immoral or godless person like Esau, who sold his own birthright for a single meal.*
>
> Hebrews 12:16

Jacob certainly wasn't perfect but he did value the birthright and he eventually went on to become Israel and the father of the twelve tribes of Israel. What happened to

Esau? Well, in Genesis 37:39-40, Isaac said Esau would live away from the fertile soil of the earth and he would live by the sword, serving his younger brother just as the Lord told Rebekah when she was pregnant with the twins. Esau went on to marry a daughter of Ishmael (ref. Genesis 28:9). Look what it also says in Hebrews concerning Esau;

> *For you know that even afterwards, when he desired to inherit the blessing, he was rejected, for he found no place for repentance, though he sought for it with tears.*
>
> Hebrews 12:17

Tragic indeed!

It is interesting to note that Abraham's second son, Isaac, also received the blessing of the firstborn. Then, Isaac's second son Jacob received the blessing of the firstborn. Then, Jacob's son Joseph was not his firstborn, but Joseph received the blessing. David was the youngest of his family and he received a blessing beyond any of his brothers by becoming king of Israel and from whom Jesus came.

In the Prodigal Son story, the older son (the son with the birthright) possessed a slave mentality and did not have the mindset of a son. Therefore, he thought like a slave, hung out with slaves and acted like a slave. As a result, he never tapped into the blessing of the firstborn or his inheritance. It wasn't stolen nor was it taken away by his father, he forfeited it. He handed it over just like Adam and Eve did. In the void created by the older son, the younger son stepped into it and was restored by his father in a place of honor and authority within the family by the robe, ring and sandals his father placed on him. Those who value the birthright and blessing of the firstborn possess the mindset of a son. Those who despise it possess a slave mentality and therefore live without it.

Very tragic indeed!

Notice how often in scripture that it wasn't the firstborn who ended up with the blessing of inheritance. God is wanting us to know that Jesus shares His inheritance with all who are born into the family of God, both male and female. We are truly co-heirs with Jesus!

It is our choice to receive it or hand it over.

8

WHAT'S IN A NAME?

NAMES ARE VERY IMPORTANT TO GOD. A name describes the nature, purpose, function and/or character of a thing or person. It also conveys the authority to accomplish it. One of the first things God had Adam do was to name all the animals. God is very careful about the names He chooses to call things, especially His people. We see this in many places in scripture.

God was very specific that Joseph and Mary were to name their child Jesus. For example; the name Jesus means "Savior and Deliverer," which is His purpose and function. Along with purpose, however, comes the God-given authority to accomplish His purpose and function. This is why we pray in the name of Jesus, which means to pray in submission to His authority and will. When we pray according to His will, our prayers have the power of His authority behind them to accomplish what we have spoken.

God had a plan all along and He revealed it in scripture beginning with Genesis. He planned a family. The Bible begins with a family and it ends with a family. God's original plan was to have sons and daughters—a family dynasty, a family of priests and kings ruling and reigning with Him for all eternity.

Let's take a look at the covenant He made with Abraham and Sarah (Genesis 17).

God changed Abram's name to Abraham and Sarai's name to Sarah. This is significant as this covenant includes all those who have received Christ by faith and become sons and daughters of God. Like us! This is our heritage. Verses 5 through 8 of chapter 17 says:

> *"No longer shall your name be called Abram, but your name shall be Abraham, for I have made you the father of a multitude of nations. I will make you exceedingly fruitful, and I will make nations of you, and kings will come forth from you. "I will establish My covenant between Me and you and your descendants after you throughout their generations for an everlasting covenant, to be God to you and to your descendants after you. "I will give to you and to your descendants after you, the land of your sojournings, all the land of Canaan, for an everlasting possession; and I will be their God."*
> Genesis 17:5-8

Then God initiates circumcision (verse 10) as the sign of the covenant. Circumcision, as I mentioned earlier, is a cutting around, a removal of flesh and it is also performed in the reproductive organ of the male by whom the identity of the child is determined. This circumcision is also a foreshadow of the circumcision of the heart that would come about as a result of Jesus' crucifixion and resurrection.

The name Abram means "exalted father." But the name Abraham means "exalted father of a multitude." By changing Abram's name, God gave Abraham a new purpose and function along with the authority and ability to accomplish it, even before Abraham had a son. Circumcision is performed in the flesh, and it is also a prophetic sign of reproducing a type of people. What type of people does God say? He said kings will come forth from him. A nation of kings! A nation of kings bound together by covenant. God chose Abraham to be the father of faith through whom a new nation of kings come.

Then God speaks about Sarai. In verse 15 and 16, God says He is changing Sarai's name to Sarah. Then God said to Abraham:

> *"As for Sarai your wife, you shall not call her name Sarai, but Sarah shall be her name. I will bless her, and indeed I will give you a son by her. Then I will bless her, and she shall be a mother of nations; kings of peoples will come from her."*
>
> Genesis 17:15-16

As mentioned previously, God has specific reasons for changing someone's name. Let's take a closer look at this name change. The name Sarai means "my princess." Sarai becomes Sarah, which now means "my prevailing princess of a multitude." Notice that God says a particular type of people will come from Sarah, that she shall be a mother of nations and kings of peoples will come from her. *Kings* are to come from her! That is plural *kings*, and a nation of them—a royal family line. He said the same thing to Abraham. God promises Abraham and Sarah that a new nation of kings, a royal family, will come from them, beginning with their promised son Isaac. In Revelation 1:5, Jesus is also referred to as the ruler of the "kings" of the earth. These kings are His people!

The name Sarah is fascinating, let's take a deeper look. *Sarah* was a word before it became a proper name. As a name, Sarah means "my princess". As a word, it means "to prevail, to persist, to contend and to persevere." As a mother of nations and kings of people, Sarah is a prevailing princess of a multitude. In Hebrew, the word sarah is the root word for government: *misrah*, meaning "to prevail, to have power like a prince, dominion, government."

Hebrew doesn't have vowels and so the word misrah would look like this transliterated: MSRH. Sarah is SRH. As you can see, there is only one letter difference between the two words. The word for government, *misrah*, is derived from the word *sarah*. Abraham, exalted father of a multitude, is a prophetic type of God the Father and one reason why he is referred to as father Abraham. Sarah is a prophetic type of the Bride of Christ, the governmental people representing the Kingdom of Heaven on earth. When God and His Bride come together in intimacy, a nation of kings is produced—a peculiar people, a holy nation of kings.

Abraham and Sarah give birth to Isaac. Isaac gives birth to Jacob and God changes his name to Israel. In Genesis 32:28, God said, "Your name shall no longer be Jacob, but Israel; for you have striven with God and with men and have prevailed." The word for *prevailed* in this passage is the word *sarah*. Because Jacob would not give up as he wrestled with the Lord until he was blessed, God gives him a new name, Israel. Israel means "he who strives with God." Israel is a compound name. The two words that make up Israel are *el* and *sarah*. *El* means "he will rule as God."

Israel, the new nation of a governmental peculiar holy people (kings), is the result of intimacy between God (Abraham) and His bride (Sarah). This also refers back to Genesis and the creation story when God blessed man to be fruitful and multiply, fill the earth, subdue it and rule over it. This has always been God's plan.

Jacob gives birth to the twelve tribes of Israel. David, which means "beloved" comes from the tribe of Judah, one of the twelve tribes. God decreed that through David and his bloodline, there will forever be a king who sits on the throne. Jesus came from the line of David, the Beloveds, and we come from the line of Jesus.

9

MY BELOVED

Beloved; [bih-luhv-id] To love greatly, dearly and well. Adored, treasured, highly esteemed and cherished. To prefer and be affectionate toward.

THIS TOPIC IS WORTHY of an entire book by itself. However, I must at least mention it in context with our new identity. We know Father God called Jesus "My beloved Son." We know Jesus is greatly loved by the Father, that He is treasured, cherished, dearly and well loved. We get that, and it is easy to understand.

But for me? Does God feel the same way about me? Does He call me beloved? Is that how He views me and feels about me…really? That's more difficult to comprehend. Well, who is God speaking about in this passage of scripture?

> *As He says also in Hosea,*
> "I WILL CALL THOSE WHO WERE NOT MY PEOPLE, 'MY PEOPLE,' AND HER WHO WAS NOT **BELOVED**, '**BELOVED**.' AND IT SHALL BE THAT IN THE PLACE WHERE IT WAS SAID TO THEM, 'YOU ARE NOT MY PEOPLE,' THERE THEY SHALL BE CALLED SONS OF THE LIVING GOD."
> Romans 9:25-26 (emphasis added)

Not hard to figure out, is it? He is speaking about us! (Assuming you have received Jesus and have become a child of God.) Just like Jesus, He calls us beloved, dearly loved, valued, adored, treasured and highly esteemed in whom He is affectionate towards! Wow! This is how the Lord views us. This is how He thinks about us, it is not dependent on our behavior. You see, from our perspective, it is all about the Lord. But from His perspective, it is all about us. That is why He sent Jesus, to redeem us! This is what covenant is all about.

Those who have been chosen of God, holy and beloved.

Think of it, He made the entire world and all it contains…for us. Every animal, bird, fish, ocean, mountain, stream, meadow, flower, tree, bush, snow, rain, color, etc., all for us, His beloved, to enjoy!

Several years ago, my wife and I celebrated a close friend's 50th birthday and joined him and his wife in the Caribbean on a scuba diving trip. We just happened to be there during the time glow worms are active, which is just for a couple of days after a full moon. Female glow worms release eggs that float to the surface of the water. The eggs give off a green light that pulsates. These pulses of light are the signal for the male worms to dart among the eggs to fertilize them. This only lasts for about fifteen minutes and is visible on the surface of the ocean. However, under the water while scuba diving at night, it is an amazing sight to see. I felt like I was floating in an underwater planetarium. When we returned to the boat, we talked about the incredible creative God we serve and how blessed we were to witness these glow worms in action and all the other creatures we saw while diving. We talked about how God created a whole universe of creatures in and under the sea, knowing that man would eventually develop a way to breathe underwater and get to see what He had created up close. He did it just for us, His beloved! He is such an amazing God and Father! We have so many experiences like this, as I am sure you do as well. God delights in us, His children, enjoying life and His creation. God loves us so much and is so affectionate towards us! He loves just hanging out with us and sharing life together.

The word *beloved* is in the Bible (NASB) 110 times; 69 times in the Old Testament and 41 times in the New Testament. The entire Book of the Song of Solomon speaks to the truth of the beloved. God's love letter to His Beloved! Thirty-one times the word beloved is mentioned in this one book alone. Here is just a small sample of the sixty-one times this word appears in the New Testament.

> "BEHOLD, MY SERVANT WHOM I HAVE CHOSEN; MY **BELOVED** IN WHOM MY SOUL IS WELL-PLEASED; I WILL PUT MY SPIRIT UPON HIM, AND HE SHALL PROCLAIM JUSTICE TO THE GENTILES."
> Matthew 12:18 (emphasis added)

> *Therefore be imitators of God, as* **beloved** *children; ...*
> Ephesians 5:1 (emphasis added)

> *... to all who are* **beloved** *of God in Rome, called as saints: Grace to you and peace from God our Father and the Lord Jesus Christ.*
> Romans 1:7 (emphasis added)

*From the standpoint of the gospel they are enemies for your sake, but from the standpoint of God's choice they are **beloved** for the sake of the fathers;*
Romans 11:28 (emphasis added)

*Therefore, my **beloved**, flee from idolatry.*
1 Corinthians 10:14 (emphasis added)

*Therefore, my **beloved** brethren, be steadfast, immovable, always abounding in the work of the Lord, knowing that your toil is not in vain in the Lord.*
1 Corinthians 15:58 (emphasis added)

*Therefore, having these promises, **beloved**, let us cleanse ourselves from all defilement of flesh and spirit, perfecting holiness in the fear of God.*
2 Corinthians 7:1 (emphasis added)

*Therefore, my **beloved** brethren whom I long to see, my joy and crown, in this way stand firm in the Lord, my beloved.*
Philippians 4:1 (emphasis added)

*… to the praise of the glory of His grace, which He freely bestowed on us in the **Beloved**.*
Ephesians 1:6 (emphasis added)

*So, as those who have been chosen of God, holy and **beloved**, put on a heart of compassion, kindness, humility, gentleness and patience; …*
Colossians 3:12 (emphasis added)

*... knowing, brethren **beloved** by God, His choice of you; ...*
    1 Thessalonians 1:4 (emphasis added)

*But we should always give thanks to God for you, brethren **beloved** by the Lord, because God has chosen you from the beginning for salvation through sanctification by the Spirit and faith in the truth.*
    2 Thessalonians 2:13 (emphasis added)

*Those who have believers as their masters must not be disrespectful to them because they are brethren, but must serve them all the more, because those who partake of the benefit are believers and **beloved**. Teach and preach these principles.*
    1 Timothy 6:2 (emphasis added)

*But, **beloved**, we are convinced of better things concerning you, and things that accompany salvation, though we are speaking in this way.*
    Hebrews 6:9 (emphasis added)

*Do not be deceived, my **beloved** brethren.*
    James 1:16 (emphasis added)

*Jude, a bond-servant of Jesus Christ, and brother of James, To those who are the called, **beloved** in God the Father, and kept for Jesus Christ: ...*
    Jude 1:1 (emphasis added)

Do you think God is trying to get our attention by putting the word beloved in scripture one hundred and ten times? I believe He is! I hope each time you come across this word, beloved, as you are reading scripture that it comes alive for you and you receive it in your heart.

When Jesus came up out of the water after being baptized by John the Baptist, God the Father spoke

> *"This is My beloved Son, in whom I am well-pleased."*
>
> Matthew 3:17

What was Jesus doing? He was just being a son. He not only loves us; He likes us and enjoys being with us!

Yet notice: Jesus hadn't preached one message yet. He hadn't performed one miracle or even picked His twelve disciples yet. The only things He did were submit to His parents, learn, grow and then get water baptized. And God called Him (as He does us): "My beloved Son in whom I am well-pleased."

What was Jesus doing? He was just being a son.

God declared that Jesus was His beloved Son two times; once at His baptism and once at His Transfiguration.

> *While he was still speaking, a bright cloud overshadowed them, and behold, a voice out of the cloud said, "This is My beloved Son, with whom I am well-pleased; listen to Him!"*
>
> Matthew 17:5

My Beloved

Both times God said it out loud so all that were present could hear.

We do not have to perform for the Lord for Him to love us or be affectionate towards us. He is not a god who is far off; He's not a statue on a table or a picture on the wall. He is alive and dwells on the inside of us. He created us for an intimate union. He not only loves us; He *likes* us and enjoys being with us!

Several times in his gospel letter the disciple John referred to himself as, "the disciple whom Jesus loved" (John 19, 20, 21). John loved Jesus very much because Jesus first loved him. Even at a very young age John saw himself as a beloved. During the Last Supper we see John laying his head on the bosom of Jesus (John 13:23). Many years later Jesus chose none other than John the beloved to author the extensive and deep revelation of Himself in the last book of the Bible; The Revelation of Jesus Christ.

It takes a beloved to kill giants and rule nations!

David was the second king of Israel, and interestingly, his name means "beloved." David wasn't sinless. He sinned greatly. He committed adultery and had the woman's husband killed to cover up his deed, to name one of his many sins.

It's fascinating to me that when we think of David, we do not think about his sin first. We typically think of him as a man after the heart of God, a great king, worshiper and warrior. Yes, he was all those things.

David is a key patriarch in scripture, hence the phrase: "Key of David." There are two scriptural references to the Key of David: Isaiah 22:22 and Revelation 3:7. To understand the Key of David" is to understand who David was, especially as a beloved son. All of the aspects of his character and who he was as a worshiper, shepherd, warrior, king and lover of God is important to understanding the Key of David. For our study here, to know him as the beloved, and that Jesus came forth from his family line, are important because this is our family line as well.

Reading the story of David's childhood (ref. 1 Samuel 16) it doesn't appear he was loved much by his family or anyone else for that matter. But David loved God and I believe he knew he was loved by God. Jesus, the beloved son of God, King of all Kings, came from the ancestral line of King David the beloved. God decreed that through David, the beloved and his bloodline will forever be a king on the throne. Jesus is the eternal King who sits on that throne. Through the new birth in Christ, we are offspring of the royal bloodline of beloveds! We belong to a beloved family dynasty.

When we are loved it gives us courage, confidence, value, inner rest and peace.

It takes a beloved to kill giants and rule nations!

10

CHANGING OUR MINDSET

OUR NEW BIRTH is just the beginning of our new life. Once we are born into the family of God, we need to renew our minds and pursue Christ-likeness. The Greek word *sozo* means "salvation." Salvation has multiple meanings. It can refer to a one-time occurrence, but it also can refer to being carried safely through to the end (preserved). Jesus put it another way: "He who endures to the end shall be saved" (Matthew 24:13). Further, we are to stay in the place of salvation to the end. Jesus said to abide in the vine. To abide means to dwell there, to stay in that place or condition. So, we are saved and we are also being saved. When we are born again, our spirit is saved and our soul (mind, will and emotions) needs to be transformed. In a matter of speaking, our soul is being saved as we renew our mind on the Word of God and obey its instruction. James 1:21 tells us, ...*in humility receive the word implanted, which is able to save your souls.* We are also in need of salvation daily from certain circumstances like traumatic events or sickness, etc.

Pursuing Christ-likeness is the transformation process (metamorphosis) of our soul. Transforming into Christ-like character is the result of being a true disciple. The Apostle Paul put it this way: "I labor among you until

Christ is formed in you" (Galatians 4:19). This is not a transformation of our spirit but of our soul. Our spirit was already made new at the new birth. Christ-like character is our greatest defense from the enemy and is the armor of God spoken of in Ephesians 6:11; "Put on the full armor of God, so that you will be able to stand firm against the schemes of the devil."

Jesus spoke at length about character. The fruit of the Spirit: love, joy, peace, patience, kindness, goodness, faithfulness, gentleness, and self-control, is Christ-likeness and is the result of intimacy with the Him. This is the fruit the Father is looking for. Sadly, it seems to be sorely missing today.

Have you noticed that we still may have addictions, habits, hurts, wounds, wrong perceptions and other things after we are born again? The born-again experience is similar to being born in the natural. When a baby is in the womb, she is in complete darkness and totally dependent on her mother for everything. When the baby is born, she comes out into the light and her whole world changes. She begins to breathe on her own and all her natural senses — sight, smell, touch, hearing and taste — are activated dramatically. However, she is still a baby. There is a lot of growing and learning to do...and choices to make. How the baby lived in the womb doesn't work outside the womb (which is probably why babies enter this world screaming.)

It is just as dramatic for all who are born again. Colossians 1:13 says: "For He rescued us from the domain of darkness and transferred us to the kingdom of His beloved Son." We are no longer under the law of sin and death but under the law of the Spirit of Life in Christ Jesus. We are in a different kingdom with a much different King and a completely different law. There is a false belief that when we are born again, we are saved and that is all there is to it.

Thank God for the born-again experience. Yet there is so much more to our life with Christ than initial salvation. God desires that all people first be born again and then be transformed in the image of His Son, Christ Jesus, through the manifestation of Christ-like character traits.

This requires our cooperation for a transformation of our soul. A disciple is a "disciplined one" in the ways of Christ Jesus—one who follows and learns from Jesus so he can be like Him. This is who we are.

As mentioned earlier, the three distinct parts of our being are spirit, soul and body. God desires that our entire being, all three parts, be sanctified and made whole.

Thank God for the born-again experience. Yet there is so much more to our life with Christ than initial salvation.

Now may the God of peace Himself sanctify you entirely; and may your spirit and soul and body be preserved complete, without blame at the coming of our Lord Jesus Christ.

1 Thessalonians 5:23

Prior to our new birth in Christ, we were by nature children of wrath (ref. Ephesians 2:3). The word for nature is *phusis*, which can be translated "lineage, to bring forth, produce." When Adam sinned, a literal change in his nature took place, and from there, nothing but sin could be produced in every part of his being—spirit, soul and body. The *zoe* life of God had departed and man was now receiving instructions from his corrupted soul (mind, will and emotions) and not from the Spirit of God as God intended.

These three parts of our being need to be addressed differently for our healing and wholeness. The spirit is reborn at the new birth and instantly is created in the image of God and according to His likeness. Thank God we will receive a new body in the resurrection and death will be conquered forever. Until then, the body needs to be disciplined, forced into submission. Apostle Paul said, "I discipline my body and make it my slave, so that, after I have preached to others, I myself will not be disqualified" 1 Cor. 9:27." The soul also needs to be transformed by the renewing of the mind. Our soul (mind, will and emotions) was programmed to think, feel and respond according to the dictates of our corrupted nature, which is dominated by the nature of the god of this world, Satan. The devil's nature can be summed up in one word: *pride*. Pride is the exaltation of self. I call it the self-life. In other words, man was trapped in a world revolving around self—what I want, what makes me feel good...me...me...me. This is humanism. Humanism is a view of life that places man at the center of life as his own god. Therefore the self-life is a life that is dictated by the natural realm: "For all that is in the world, the lust of the flesh and the lust of the eyes and the boastful pride of life, is not from the Father, but is from the world" (1 John 2).

> *Do not love the world, nor the things in the world. If anyone loves the world, the love of the Father is not in him. For all that is in the world,*

Changing Our Mindset

> *the lust of the flesh and the lust of the eyes and the boastful pride of life, is not from the Father, but is from the world. The world is passing away, and also its lusts; but the one who does the will of God lives forever.*
>
> 1 John 2:15-17

The devil's nature can be summed up in one word: pride.

Our soul has been trained to live by the lust of the flesh, lust of the eyes and the boastful pride of life. In fact, pride is at the core of all sin. We have learned to live by our natural senses, our desires, our emotions, and what we determine is right and wrong. This is a consequence of eating from the wrong tree, and it has been devastating to us. Note that the tree at the center of man's fall is not called "the tree of evil," but "the tree of the knowledge of good and evil." It has led man to determine for himself what is good and what is evil and to reject God's word.

In contrast to the tendencies of sinful man, Jesus, when tempted by the devil to turn rocks into bread, replied succinctly:

> *But He answered [the devil] and said, "It is written, 'Man shall not live on bread alone, but on every word that proceeds out of the mouth of God.'"*
>
> Matthew 4:4 (emphasis mine)

Bread is natural, physical, food. We need it to live in a natural world. Of course, Jesus was not saying to avoid food. Rather, He was saying to not live by the natural *alone* but also by the Word (rhema) of God. Another way to say this is not to live by the soul alone but by every word that proceeds from the mouth of God.

Sadly, many Christians still live by the natural (or unsanctified soul), not by the spirit. This affects how they pray, how they speak and what they focus their attention on. It makes it impossible to see or perceive from the spirit (ref. 2 Cor. 2:14).

This is why so many people have a hard time seeing themselves as God does. They struggle to understand scripture, how the Holy Spirit is leading them, the voice of God and so much more. Their mind is trapped in the natural. Sin has left its devastating mark of corruption on their souls— their thinking, desires and emotions. Yet God gave us everything we need to rectify this. This is a reason why it is common to believe that we have two natures—the old man and the new man within us, and that we are still sinners. We have a new spirit but our soul needs transforming to align with the spirit.

So, how can we escape this pervasive corruption? Simple! The old programming of our soul must be erased and new programming installed (to use computer lingo). We begin the process of renewing our minds by studying and meditating on the written Word of God and do what it says to do. This aligns our soul with the Spirit of God and we begin to know the mind of the Christ.

> *But you did not learn Christ in this way, if indeed you have heard Him and have been taught in Him, just as truth is in Jesus, that, in reference to your former manner of life, you lay aside the old self, which is being corrupted in*

> *accordance with the lusts of deceit, and that you be renewed in the spirit of your mind, and put on the new self, which in the likeness of God has been created in righteousness and holiness of the truth.*
>
> Ephesians 4:20-24

Notice this scripture is exhorting us to be renewed in the spirit of our mind. We are to put on the new self, which is living according to our new identity. It doesn't say to pray about it or ask God to do it for us. We must change our mindset and think differently so that we will speak differently and behave differently, becoming more Christ-like in character day by day.

> *And do not be conformed to this world, but be transformed by the renewing of your mind, that you may prove what the will of God is, that which is good and acceptable and perfect.*
>
> Romans 12:2

When God tells us to do something, the grace (or enabling power) of God comes along with it. We just respond in faith and do what He says. Again, this scripture is telling us to do something, to not be conformed to the world but instead, be transformed by renewing our minds. This is our responsibility, not God's. The word *conformed* means "to be pressed or squeezed into a mold, to be fashioned." The world tries to shape and fashion us according to who they think we should be. We are to resist the world's influence along with its philosophies and beliefs to press us into their mold even if it comes from a preacher or other Christians.

This conforming work by the world is an external work. We are to resist being shaped by external circumstances and situations when they contradict scripture. As we study and meditate on God's Word and put it into practice in our lives, we will be transformed in our thinking. The word for *transformed* is the word *metamorphosis*. The work of the Spirit is an internal work of transformation that will manifest externally. This is a result of our new DNA that has been programmed by God in the new birth and fostered through cooperating with the Holy Spirit, producing the Fruit of the Spirit.

Without this process, we can learn behaviors and look good externally but inwardly we can be full of dead men's bones. Legalistic religion works on the external. At the new birth, everything according to life and godliness is given to us in seed form. It works on the internal.

> *... seeing that His divine power has granted to us everything pertaining to life and godliness, through the true knowledge of Him who called us by His own glory and excellence.*
>
> 2 Peter 1:3

> *... for you have been born again not of seed which is perishable but imperishable, that is, through the living and enduring word of God.*
>
> 1 Peter 1:23

Through renewing the mind and obeying God's Word, those seeds will grow and mature and we will be transformed more and more into the image of Christ.

OUR TRUE NATURE

Even though we still may sin, that doesn't mean we have a corrupt nature anymore, nor does it mean we are now sinners. Even after we are born again, our free will is still involved in every thought and decision we make. If I get down on all fours and bark like a dog and eat with my mouth out of a dog bowl, that doesn't make me a dog. I am capable of doing dog-like things, but I am still a human being. Likewise, even though we are children of God and have His nature within us, we can still sin but that doesn't make us a sinner. We have no excuse for our behavior any longer. There is no sin nature inside of us controlling us, only a corrupt soul that needs renewing. God has given us free choice. We must choose to exercise it.

> *Only sons are led by the Holy Spirit. Slaves are not.*

We have the nature of God within us now that we are born again. So, we need to renew our minds with His Word — both written and spoken Word — while developing our relationship with Him and yielding to the Holy Spirit in obedience. This is what it means to be led by the Spirit of God. Romans 8:14 tells us that "all who are being led by the Spirit of God, these are sons of God." Only sons are led by the Holy Spirit. Slaves are not.

We can truly live as Jesus lived. It is our choice. Do we want to be a son? To think and live as a son? Or will we choose to think and live like a slave? Slaves by definition are in bondage. They are ruled and controlled by someone or something. As with the older son in the Prodigal son story, he was controlled by a false mindset (a corrupt soul). His slave mentality dictated his thoughts and therefore his emotions, words, actions and worldview. It is not the truth that will control us, it is what we believe to be truth.

> *For those who are according to the flesh set their minds on the things of the flesh* (natural), *but those who are according to the Spirit, the things of the Spirit. For the mind set on the flesh* (natural) *is death, but the mind set on the Spirit is life and peace, because the mind set on the flesh is hostile toward God; for it does not subject itself to the law of God, for it is not even able to do so, and those who are in the flesh cannot please God.*
>
> Romans 8:5-8 (parenthesis added)

> *Since you have in obedience to the truth purified your souls for a sincere love of the brethren, fervently love one another from the heart, for you have been born again not of seed which is perishable but imperishable, that is, through the living and enduring word of God.*
>
> 1 Peter 1:22-23

A key message from this passage is that obedience to the truth purifies our soul. Incredible!

IDENTITY AND HEALING

The truth about your identity in Christ is the foundation for your healing process. A godly sense of identity will cause you to see and think about yourself as God does. It is not who you *think* you are that will make the difference. It is who you *know* you are. We need to know that sin, sickness and disease are NOT part of our identity any longer as sons and daughters of God! Can you imagine thinking that sin, sickness and disease are part of who Jesus is? I certainly can't! There is no scriptural proof otherwise. If these things are not part of who He is, they are not part of who we are.

The beginning to all true healing and freedom is the Word of God, and Jesus is the Word.

In the beginning was the Word, and the Word was with God, and the Word was God.

And the Word became flesh, and dwelt among us, and we saw His glory, glory as of the only begotten from the Father, full of grace and truth.

John 1:1, 1:14

We need to know what the written Word of God says, and we also need to hear the spoken Word of God for our personal situation. The written Word (*logos*) is for all people in all places at all times. No matter who we are, where we live or what age we live in, the written Word of God is for you. The spoken Word (*rhema*) can be more personal. We need personal direction, advice and counsel. The Holy Spirit will speak to us directly, through others, or in a variety of other ways. Jesus healed people but He did so differently. Healing is for everyone but how to receive that healing is specific for each individual. God relates to each of us on a personal level and it always requires faith.

Seeing and Hearing

Our mind sees in pictures or images. Our imagination is very powerful. God created our minds to work by seeing — the ability to see with our mind's eye. Now, don't get worried. This is not new-age religion, mind over matter nor witchcraft. Seeing with the mind's eye needs to come from God's word, not our thoughts, opinions, human reasonings and vain imaginations. Jesus is the Word and as we behold or "see" Him we are transformed into His image.

> *But we all, with unveiled face, beholding as in a mirror the glory of the Lord, are being transformed into the same image from glory to glory, just as from the Lord, the Spirit.*
>
> 2 Corinthians 3:18

Jesus does what He sees the Father doing and He says what He hears Him saying.

Jesus said He does what He sees the Father doing and He says what He hears Him saying. This is our example to follow. We listen to God's voice no matter where or who it comes from. When we know what God said, we focus our mind on His word, hearing and seeing, so we can say and do, just like Jesus did. God has given us the ability to take every thought and imagination captive to the obedience of Christ.

> *We are destroying speculations and every lofty thing raised up against the knowledge of God, and we are taking every thought captive to the obedience of Christ, ...*
>
> 2 Corinthians 10:5

The battlefield is our mind — our thought life. Our thoughts, attitudes, opinions, imaginations and beliefs can become strongholds within us. It doesn't matter whether they are true or not. What we believe to be true makes all the difference. Our beliefs control our perspective on life—how we feel, speak and behave. These thoughts are fortresses or strongholds in our mind that need to be taken captive to the obedience of Christ. We are instructed to take every thought captive. Not just the sinful thoughts or negative ones but every thought - good, bad or indifferent. Yes, there are even some good thoughts that are not in agreement with the Lord—thoughts that are actually hindering us

> *For though we walk in the flesh, we do not war according to the flesh, for the weapons of our warfare are not of the flesh, but divinely powerful for the destruction of fortresses [strongholds]. We are destroying speculations and every lofty thing raised up against the knowledge of God, and we are taking every thought captive to the obedience of Christ, and we are ready to punish all disobedience, whenever your obedience is complete.*
> 2 Corinthians 10:3-6 (emphasis added)

The mind is where spiritual warfare is fought. If all you can see is sickness, disease, sin or lack, you must learn to take those thoughts and images captive, begin thinking like Christ and seeing yourself as He sees you. The Holy Spirit is not our Doer. He is our Helper. He will help us destroy these strongholds that are built upon speculations, vain imaginations, bad teaching, false beliefs and every lofty thing raised up against the knowledge of God. But we cannot just pray about this and ask God to do it for us. Our part in this transformation is to take control of our thought life and submit it to His truth

> *So Jesus was saying to those Jews who had believed Him, "If you continue in My word, then you are truly disciples of Mine; and you will know the truth, and the truth will make you free."*
>
> John 8:31-32

Jesus did not say the truth will make you free. He said if we continue in His word, we will know the truth and then the truth will make us free. Truth alone doesn't make us free; we must know the truth and live according to the truth. The truth is much more than a concept. The truth is a person: Jesus Christ. Freedom and healing begin and end with Him. When we receive Him and follow Him in all His ways, being obedient to His words, we will be free to be all God has created us to be!

Do not settle for anything less.

TREATING SYMPTOMS VS CAUSES

Much of the world's system of healing is not true, complete healing. The prescription drug therapy and learned behaviors offered by so many treat the symptoms and cover the pain but never deal directly with the root cause of the pain. Merely teaching coping skills overlooks the complete and total healing that God wants to bring us—healing that cures not only the outward behaviors but also the deep roots that cause our behaviors. Thank God for doctors and medicine who help and cure certain sicknesses and diseases. Advances in medicine and medical practices have come a long way. But still, doctors cannot heal everything, God can.

For example, within the world's system of healing, an alcoholic seeking help is often told they will always be an alcoholic, that alcoholism is a disease they will need to learn to live with. Even in Alcoholics Anonymous, which has helped so many quit drinking and stay sober, the person still introduces himself weekly by saying, "Hi, I'm Jack. I'm an alcoholic." By confessing week after week, a negative identity instead of speaking God's definition of himself, Jack is held in bondage to a destructive pattern and view of himself. So even though he may be taught skills that keep him from drinking, he is not totally free from addiction because he is not delivered from the root cause. Often, the root of addiction surfaces in another area. Family members can testify that the drinking behavior may have indeed stopped, but the victim is still addicted to other behaviors like outbursts of anger, over-eating or compulsive smoking.

GENERATIONAL CURSES AND FAMILY HISTORY

We are often asked to list your family history when visiting a doctor? Why? Because statistics show that a certain sickness or disease may be a family trait and therefore, we have a higher risk of contracting it. This is an example of a generational curse.

However, there are many more. Yes, we may have a high risk of contracting a certain disease that runs in our family bloodline but as a child of God, we belong to another bloodline! We do not have to accept the curses that run in our biological family! Those curses can stop with us! God always goes to the root of the problem, plucks it out and brings true healing and freedom for us and our future generations. "So if the Son makes you free, you will be free indeed" (John 8:36).

Before I was born again, I was addicted to marijuana and other drugs including alcohol. In the world's system, once you're an alcoholic or drug abuser, you will always be an alcoholic or a drug abuser. But when God sets us free, we are totally free. That is what happened to me. I can humbly and joyfully proclaim that addiction is no longer part of my identity. It is not who I am. I do not have symptoms, cravings or desires for those things any longer. I don't need to learn coping skills in order to deal with something that is no longer a part of who I am.

Never settle for learning coping skills to deal with symptoms. Always be willing to go to the root of the problem and allow it to be plucked out by the power of God. His divine power has granted to us everything pertaining to life and godliness through the true knowledge of Him who called us by His own glory and excellence (2 Peter 1:3).

> *Blessed be the God and Father of our Lord Jesus Christ, who according to His great mercy has caused us to be born again to a living hope through the resurrection of Jesus Christ from the dead, to obtain an inheritance which is imperishable and undefiled and will not fade away, reserved in heaven for you, who are protected by the power of God through faith for a salvation ready to be revealed in the last time.*
>
> 1 Peter 1:3-5

Jesus is more than enough to deliver us and set us free from whatever is holding us captive or causing sickness or disease. Jesus is anointed to proclaim release, and He transferred that same anointing to us!

> *"The Spirit of the Lord is upon Me, because He anointed Me to preach the gospel to the poor. He has sent Me to proclaim release to the captives, and recovery of sight to the blind, to set free those who are oppressed to proclaim the favorable year of the Lord."*
>
> Luke 4:18-19

It is not a matter of whether God wants to heal us or not. That may be the first stumbling block you will have to overcome. If you do not believe God wants to heal you, or if you believe that He has made you sick to teach you a lesson, improve your character or help others you will never be free.

If God truly puts sickness on us to teach us something, then why was Jesus never sick? After all, Jesus was the smartest person to have ever lived and his character was flawless. Yet we never see an example of Jesus causing a person to become sick in order to teach them a lesson. In fact, we see the opposite. The Bible tells us that Jesus spent His time "doing good and healing all who were oppressed by the devil" as well as healing all manner of sickness and disease (ref. Acts 10:38). If we believe God makes people suffer through sickness, yet sent Jesus to cure sickness, it seems that Jesus and God are working against each other. That doesn't even make sense.

The question we should ask ourselves is not *if* God wants to heal us but *how* He wants to heal us. Jesus healed people in many different ways. To some, He spoke a word. To others, He cast out demons. Still others, He said, "Stop sinning lest something worse come upon you." One time, He spit in the dirt to make mud, put it on a man's eyes and told him to go wash. When he washed off the mud, the man began to see. Another time, a woman touched the hem of His robe and she was healed of a bleeding issue even though Jesus didn't know who had touched him.

> *Faith is acting on what God says, not believing what we want to believe.*

In all cases, faith was required. Faith consists of hearing and knowing what God is saying and then doing what He says. Faith is not convincing yourself enough that something is going to happen and then believing that. That borders on witchcraft. Rather, faith is placing confidence and trust in God. Therefore, faith is initiated when we know what His will is in any given situation. Faith is acting on what God says, not believing what we want to believe.

Sometimes just a word spoken by our Father can set us free, whether it comes from Him directly or through another person.

A couple of years after I was born again, I still struggled with low self-esteem. I wasn't comfortable being myself. I was self-conscious. This was a bondage that I needed deliverance from.

One afternoon as I was riding my motorcycle, the Lord spoke to me concerning this issue. What He said was simple and short but so powerful because it was God who said it. I haven't been the same since. He simply said, "Be yourself." Those two words hit my heart and set me free! Amazing!

Sometimes we need to hear a word from God and then speak it over ourselves. Or He may tell us something to do or to stop doing.

Another time in my life my kidneys were producing kidney stones. They are extremely painful. I had five separate occurrences of them in a short period of time. My mother had also suffered from kidney stones most of her adult life, and my brother had a kidney stone as well. This was obviously a generational curse, but I decided I wasn't going to accept it any longer. So, I asked the Lord what to do about it. He gave me three instructions: I was to:

1. Take two different vitamin supplements.
2. Cut down on my salt intake.
3. Speak to my body to tell it to stop producing kidney stones.

I did what He said, and I haven't had another stone since.

Now, if you have kidney stones, don't do what God told me to do. Each person is unique (just like everyone else). Our body chemistries are also unique. You need to hear from God for yourself. Most people just want an easy fix. They want someone to pray for them and make the problem go away without changing their lifestyle or taking the time to hear God speak to them individually.

God has a way to heal you, and you need to hear what He is saying to you specifically and then do it.

That is faith.

There are different reasons why people become sick. They may be using a toxic chemical at home or work. Or they may be eating or drinking something that is negatively affecting their bodies. In these cases, the answer may simply be a change in diet, lifestyle or environment.

Most of our automobiles run on gasoline or diesel. We cannot put whatever we want in the fuel tank and expect it to run. Our bodies are the same way. They are more complex than an automobile engine and are designed to function with the proper amount of water along with the right foods, vitamins and minerals. If we are not eating correctly, our bodies will suffer the consequences. They will get sick and break down. This is not a mystery. It is simple, straightforward logic. That is why we need to hear from the Lord on an individual basis. We must learn the answer for our particular healing. Then, we must do what He says, so that we may be healed.

It is an absolute necessity that we renew our minds with the Word of God.

> *And do not be conformed to this world, but be transformed by the renewing of your mind, so that you may prove what the will of God is, that which is good and acceptable and perfect.*
>
> Romans 12:2

Changing Our Mindset

We must change the way we think. We also need to discipline ourselves and learn to recognize the voice of God.

> *All Scripture is inspired by God and profitable for teaching, for reproof, for correction, for training in righteousness; so that the man of God may be adequate, equipped for every good work.*
> 2 Timothy 3:16-17

Hearing the word of God preached or even reading it for ourselves is not enough. It is not the same thing as doing it. It will not have the same effect on our lives. God has a purpose for each of us, and if we are in bondage to sin, sickness, disease, generational curses or fleshly mindsets, we will be hindered from fulfilling God's ultimate purpose and destiny.

> *For if anyone is a hearer of the word and not a doer, he is like a man who looks at his natural face in a mirror; for once he has looked at himself and gone away, he has immediately forgotten what kind of person he was. But one who looks intently at the perfect law, the law of liberty, and abides by it, not having become a forgetful hearer but an effectual doer, this man will be blessed in what he does.*
> James 1:23-25

Hearing the Word is great, but it is the first step. We must be *doers* of the Word! James says that as we look into the Word of God, it is like looking into a mirror. The Word is not just reflecting who Jesus is but also reflecting who God created us to be!

> *Grace and peace be multiplied to you in the knowledge of God and of Jesus our Lord; seeing that His divine power has granted to us everything pertaining to life and godliness, through the true knowledge of Him who called us by His own glory and excellence. For by these He has granted to us His precious and magnificent promises, so that by them you may become partakers of the divine nature, having escaped the corruption that is in the world by lust.*
>
> 2 Peter 1:2-4

God has given us everything that pertains to life (*zoe*) and godliness. God has already done all He is going to do. He has given all He is going to give. It is there for the taking but it comes a certain way—through the true knowledge of Jesus Christ. We can be partakers of the divine nature if we want to. This is how we will escape the corruption that is in the world by lust!

Begin to live according to who you are!

11

DOMINION

WE HAVE SPENT the majority of time in this book answering the first great question that man has sought the answer to over the ages: *Who am I?* The correct answer to this question begins to answer the next two questions.

Why am I here?

Where am I going?

"Why am I here?" speaks of our purpose. All of mankind shares a common purpose, and each individual has a personal purpose. As a child of God, our nature is the same. However, our personalities are unique, meaning that our gifts, callings and roles in life are different as well. Therefore, each of us needs to take the time to hear specifically from the Lord about our personal purpose and determine where our place is. Each of us has been created by God with unique gifts and talents. Our gifts and callings are important as they serve and build up people and help to expand the Kingdom. It is up to us to discover them and put them to work wherever God calls us for His ultimate glory and our fulfillment.

In Mark, it says that Jesus appointed twelve disciples for two main reasons. These two reasons sum up our common purpose.

> *And He appointed twelve, so that they would be with Him and that He could send them out to preach, and to have authority to cast out the demons.*
>
> Mark 3:14-15

The first reason we are appointed by the Lord is that He wants to be with us. He desires to have an intimate relationship with each one of us. His will is that all men are born again, established in an intimate relationship with Him, and are Christ-like in character (ref. John 3:16, 1 Timothy 2:4).

The second reason is that He has work for each of us to do. Actually, we have the privilege of partnering with Him in His work. Whatever your specific career field, occupation and region you live in, His work for each of us is to expand the influence of the Kingdom of Heaven by removing Satanic strongholds from people and regions, thereby making disciples of all nations.

This is very similar to what God said about our purpose during the act of creation.

> *Then God said, "Let Us make man in Our image, according to Our likeness; and let them rule over the fish of the sea and over the birds of the sky and over the cattle and over all the earth, and over every creeping thing that creeps on the earth." God created man in His own image, in the image of God He created him; male and female He created them. God blessed them; and God said to them, "Be fruitful and multiply, and fill the earth, and subdue it; and rule over the fish*

> *of the sea and over the birds of the sky and over every living thing that moves on the earth."*
> Genesis 1:26-28

Notice in verse 26 that God said, "Let us make man in our image according to our likeness and let them subdue the earth and rule..." Man's first purpose is to be created in the image of God, which means having the same nature as God and obtaining the same character as God that is revealed through Christ Jesus. We see that purpose fulfilled in Jesus.

In verse 28, God blessed man to be fruitful, multiply, fill the earth, subdue it, and rule over every living thing that moves on the earth. Each of these assignments has both a natural and a spiritual application. To be fruitful and multiply and fill the earth means to reproduce ourselves by having children. But it goes beyond the natural meaning. In the spiritual sense, we are to reproduce ourselves by making disciples of Jesus Christ as He said in Matthew 28.

> *But the eleven disciples proceeded to Galilee, to the mountain which Jesus had designated. When they saw Him, they worshiped Him; but some were doubtful. And Jesus came up and spoke to them, saying, "All authority has been given to Me in heaven and on earth. Go therefore and make disciples of all the nations, baptizing them in the name of the Father and the Son and the Holy Spirit, teaching them to observe all that I commanded you; and lo, I am with you always, even to the end of the age."*
> Matthew 28:16-20

But God also said to subdue the earth and rule over it. The word *subdue* means to bring into subjection, to conquer, to bring into bondage. This word has a sense of force. The word *rule* means to have dominion, to dominate, to prevail against. So, we can see that another part of our common purpose is to bring the entire earth and all that is on it—both people and nature—into subjection to the Lord and His will. As His ambassador sons, we are to rule by the delegated authority we receive from Him. Our purpose is to subdue the earth and rule over it by bringing the entire earth and all its created beings into the freedom and liberty that the Kingdom of Heaven provides. We do not do this by force, coercion or deception, but by love. Romans 8:19-22 hints at this when it says that the entire creation is waiting for the sons of God to manifest its freedom from corruption.

> *For the anxious longing of the creation waits eagerly for the revealing of the sons of God. For the creation was subjected to futility, not willingly, but because of Him who subjected it, in hope that the creation itself also will be set free from its slavery to corruption into the freedom of the glory of the children of God. For we know that the whole creation groans and suffers the pains of childbirth together until now.*
>
> Romans 8:19-22

Think of it: All of creation is waiting for the sons and daughters of God to be revealed. And from this, God is in the process of creating one new man out of Jews and Gentiles. This does not mean Gentiles become Jews or Jews become Gentiles. Rather, the one new man is Jew and Gentile coming into Christ-likeness. Jesus is the One New Man! Sons and daughters of God living like Christ with love for one another is the greatest witness for God that the world can see.

> *"By this all men will know that you are My disciples, if you have love for one another."*
>
> John 13:35

Jesus said the world would know we are His disciples by the love we have for one another, not by our creative events or concert style worship, nor by our charismatic preaching or fancy PowerPoints. Jesus didn't even say that the world would know we are His disciples by the signs, wonders and miracles we perform! No, He said love. Not the world's kind of love but the God kind of unconditional love. Why love? Because God is love and love is what He created us for—to receive it and to give it. Love is the most powerful force on the planet. Every person needs love. We cannot help it; it is knit into our DNA.

Everything that happens to us, every circumstance and situation we go through and all that God does in our lives has the potential to conform us to the image of Christ.

God's blessing is already on what He called us to be and to do. He has blessed us to be fruitful, multiply, fill the earth, subdue the earth and rule over it. To enter into the blessing of the Lord is to be who He created us to be and do what He has already prepared for us to do. We may ask God to come and bless what we are doing, but in reality, God's blessing is already on what He told us to be involved in. In Ephesians, it says God has already prepared good works for us to walk in.

> *For we are His workmanship, created in Christ Jesus for good works, which God prepared beforehand so that we would walk in them.*
>
> Ephesians 2:10

What are those good works?

- *Bearing* fruit in Christ-like character.
- *Multiplying* by making disciples.
- *Ruling* with Him over the earth and bringing the earth under the dominion of the King and His Kingdom.

Everything that happens to us, every circumstance and situation we go through and all that God does in our lives has the potential to conform us to the image of Christ. I am not saying that God causes all that happens in our lives; however, He will take those things and turn them for our good, (ref. Romans 8:28). It's a promise!

Another part of our common purpose is to dwell in the place that God has provided for us. In Genesis 2:8, it says that God planted a garden and placed the man there. Out of the entire earth, God placed man in a small place called the Garden of Eden. Even though God commissioned man to fill the earth and subdue it, He placed man in a small area on the earth first. In this Garden was provided everything man needed for life and godliness. God supplied food to eat, water to drink, an intimate relationship with the Lord, a spouse, an occupation, as well as nature and animals for enjoyment.

In this place, God also protected man from death which is the curse. As long as man continued in right relationship with the Lord, which included submission to His authority, then man continued to have provision, protection, authority, rest and peace.

This was the will of God, but we know this is not the way it turned out. Since God gave man delegated authority over the earth, when man sinned by obeying Satan instead of God, then man obeyed the very one he should have ruled over and the curse was released on the earth. As a result of the curse, man began to experience guilt, shame, blame, fear and loss, which in turn caused them to cover themselves and hide.

God removed man from the Garden of Eden. Man lost his position with God and his location in the Garden. Their occupation became much more difficult and skewed over time. They would work harder now and produce less. Fruitfulness and multiplication through childbearing would now be painful. Husbands would now rule over wives. Sickness, disease and ultimately death (including the aging process) would now appear.

This is just a snapshot of what happened to man as a result of his disobedience to God. The entire earth and all created things were affected by the curse.

Praise the Lord that Jesus came to restore to us all that was lost! And yet God's idea of restoration is not merely to put us back where we were or return only that which we have lost. He has a different definition of restoration than we do. His restoration propels us further than where we were and restores more to us than that which we lost! Note that the prodigal son in Luke 15 was not just restored to where he had been before he left. He was propelled to a higher stature within the family, as signified by the robe, ring and sandals given to him by his father. The story doesn't tell us that he had these things prior to leaving his father.

And how about Job? His loss was tremendous, almost unbelievable. Yet God did not restore to him exactly what he lost. Look at this passage in Job 42:10; "The LORD restored the fortunes of Job when he prayed for his friends, and the LORD increased all that Job had twofold."

Scripture says that God restored Job *twofold*. (Still one wife, though.)

The Garden of Eden is an example of the principle that God has appointed places for people to live both as nations and individuals. He called Abraham and Jacob (Israel) to a specific place. Likewise, He has called each of us to a specific city, region and country. But just as important as our physical location, He has also called us to a spiritual place.

The Garden of Eden represents a spiritual place—the Kingdom of Heaven on earth. John the Baptist came preaching "the Kingdom of Heaven." This is also what Jesus came preaching. He told us that the gospel of the Kingdom would be preached in the last days and then the end would come. We are not living in the Church Age as many say we are. We are living in the Kingdom Age. The Kingdom is now, and it is not fully come yet. The Kingdom of God will be fully manifest when Jesus returns!

The Kingdom of Heaven on earth is the place where all we need is provided.

There are many types of illustrations in the Bible that represent the Kingdom of Heaven. The Sabbath Day is one of them. We know that Sabbath Day was the seventh day of creation, the day the Lord rested from His works. He blessed the seventh day and sanctified it. He commanded His people to rest from their works on that day and to keep it holy. When recording the creation story, the Bible consistently mentions this phrase after each day's creation: "and there was evening and there was morning, one day [a second day, a third day, etc.]"

However, after the creation of the seventh day, there is no mention of evening and morning. That is because the Sabbath Day was to present a pattern of perpetual rest. This is the "Day" all believers are to dwell in. It was a picture of the salvation rest in Jesus, the millennial rest of God's people with Satan who will be bound 1,000 years, and then the ultimate rest of a new heaven and new earth with all sin destroyed.

As a matter of fact, in Genesis 2:15, it says,

> *Then the LORD God took the man and put him into the garden of Eden to cultivate it and keep it.*

The word *put* literally means, "to set at rest." Further, *cultivate* means "to serve." And *keep it* means "to watch over it, preserve it." The word *garden* means "an enclosure." The word *Eden* means "delight." So, we could read this verse this way;

> Then the Lord God took the man and set him at rest in the Garden of Delight to serve in the garden and to watch over the garden and preserve the garden.

When we are born again, we are delivered from the domain of darkness and transferred to the Kingdom of God's beloved Son. Colossians tells us:

> *For He rescued us from the domain of darkness, and transferred us to the kingdom of His beloved Son, in whom we have redemption, the forgiveness of sins.*
>
> Colossians 1:13-14

The Garden of Eden is a representation of the Kingdom of Heaven on earth, so we can read Genesis 2:15 this way:

> Then the Lord God took man and set him at rest in the Kingdom of Heaven on earth to serve in the Kingdom and to watch over the Kingdom and preserve the Kingdom.

That rendering opens a new understanding of our purpose on earth.

The Sabbath Day and the Garden of Eden are just a couple of examples of living in the Kingdom of Heaven on earth. Here are a few more among many others:

- Noah's Ark: a safe place where men and animals were provided for and protected. It also represents salvation.
- The Promised Land: a land flowing with milk and honey; full, abundant provision and victory over

enemies; also the place for God's covenant people to occupy, take dominion over, be fruitful and multiply.
- The Holy of Holies: the sacred place where the very presence of God dwelt.

When Jesus was crucified, the veil that separated people from the presence of God was torn in two. That veil is now wide open for all mankind to enter and dwell. It is not a place to come and visit, but a place to live in God's presence on earth.

Each of these things: The Garden of Eden, Noah's ark, the Promised land and the Holy of Holies is a natural example of a spiritual reality. Jesus said, "But seek first His kingdom and His righteousness, and all these things will be added to you" (Matthew 6:33). All of our needs will be taken care of if we put the Kingdom of God and Jesus' righteousness first in our lives.

This will be the end result when Jesus returns to earth.

> ... so that at the name of Jesus every knee will bow, of those who are in heaven and on earth and under the earth, and that every tongue will confess that Jesus Christ is Lord, to the glory of God the Father.
>
> Philippians 2:10-11

At the Second Coming of Christ He will set up His Kingdom and He, along with His children, will reign and rule for all eternity.

THE MASK OF A FALSE IDENTITY

Understanding who and what we are is necessary to live and function as citizens in the Kingdom of God.

If we are living under a false identity, we believe we are something other than what we truly are. This affects everything: our worldview, how we think, talk, pray and act. How we see ourselves becomes the lens through which we see the world around us and the people within it. In other words, we see the world as we are, not as it truly is.

As mentioned earlier in the book, Jesus laid out a principle for us when He said the greatest commandment is to love God and love our neighbor as we love ourselves. In other words, we will love our neighbors through the lens of love for self. How we love ourselves is the lens we use to project onto others. Understanding this will help to answer so many relationship problems we have. Obtaining a healthy, biblical love for self is having God's perspective.

Understanding who and what we are is necessary to live and function as citizens in the Kingdom of God. In Matthew 16, Jesus asked His disciples, "Who do people say that the Son of Man is?" Then He asked them directly, "But who do you say that I am?" It was after they answered His identity question correctly that He told them what He would build; His Ekklesia. Ekklesia is not church. I wrote a book about this called *Ekklesia; The Government of the Kingdom of Heaven on Earth*. The Ekklesia is much more than a group of called-out ones. The

Ekklesia is a governmental assembly, a ruling council of priests and kings on the earth. In 1 Peter 2:9, we read:

> *But you are* A CHOSEN RACE, A ROYAL PRIESTHOOD, A HOLY NATION, A PEOPLE FOR GOD'S OWN POSSESSION, *so that you may proclaim the excellencies of Him who has called you out of darkness into His marvelous light...*

It takes a beloved to conquer giants. We are beloved sons and daughters of God, priests and kings.

The word for *chosen* in this scripture means "favorite choice." The word for *race* is the same word for *genes* in English, meaning "family, offspring and a kind of species." And *royal* means "kingly or the family line of royalty." As the Ekklesia, we are the government of a holy nation, a chosen race and royal priesthood—a priesthood that is royal. A royal priesthood is a combination of priests and kings. The Ekklesia, then, is a family dynasty.

Jesus said He would build His Ekklesia, the government of the Kingdom of Heaven on earth (ref. Matthew 16).

We are a beloved family dynasty! This is our birthright. This is our heritage and our identity.

When the Father becomes one with His governmental bride, the Ekklesia, we become fruitful and multiply, producing a nation of kings that rule and reign with the Lord in righteousness and justice over the earth and for all eternity. This was God's idea, not man's.

Through faith in Christ Jesus, we are born into this family dynasty and adopted by God with the legal right to the inheritance that belongs to Jesus. The right to subdue the earth and rule over it has been restored.

When the entire Israeli army was in fear, listening to Goliath taunt them, it was a beloved, David, who entered the scene focused on the Lord and not the enemy. He did not ignore Goliath; he just chose to focus on the Lord instead. He knew God and His authority and power as well as God's covenant with His people, Israel. David, who was anointed the beloved king of Israel, overcame the giant of the day in the power and authority of Yahweh, The Creator of Heaven and earth.

It takes a beloved to conquer giants. We are beloved sons and daughters of God, priests and kings, with the privilege of being part of His family dynasty, the Ekklesia.

> *Beloved, now we are children of God, and it has not appeared as yet what we will be. We know that when He appears, we will be like Him, because we will see Him just as He is.*
>
> 1 John 3:2

This is who and what we are!

For Further Reading

For further understanding of Ekklesia and what Jesus said He would build, you can get Joe's book; *Ekklesia; The Government of the Kingdom of Heaven on Earth*, on Amazon or Apple Books.

When Jesus told His disciples in Matthew 16 that He would build His church, what would the disciples have thought He meant? Since there wasn't a church in existence, would the disciples have understood what Jesus meant? It appears they did but, how could they? This book explores what Jesus actually said He would build, how it was lost and what it means to us today.

CONTACT INFORMATION

Joe Nicola
New Covenant Ministries
Independence, Missouri

(816) 836-8303

Email: joenicola@ncmworld.com

Made in the USA
Lexington, KY
23 June 2019